Mark Yang brings together wisdom and kindness along with East and West. Science often requires us to know things definitively. But the science of therapy, especially existential therapy, instead requires us to embrace ambiguity: to let go of certainty and dwell instead in faith in our own capacities. This book is for students and masters alike whose practices require an awakening of that faith. Wu Wei is the heart of this practice—effortless action, effortful inaction.

Jason Dias, PsyD, Assistant Professor of Psychology at Pikes Peak Community College and Co-Founder of The International Institute of Existential–Humanistic Psychology

In a profession where supervision seems to have been reduced to checking documentation and reviewing legal risks, Mark Yang's, *Lighting the Candle: Taoist Principles in Clinical Supervision Practiced from an Existential–Humanistic Perspective*, comes to us as itself a true flame in the darkness, and just at the right time. Yang evokes the Taoist tradition of the narrative in teaching and learning so consistent with the existential–humanistic tradition and clears space for the beautiful paradox of Taoism in the supervisory process: doing without doing, being there while being "superfluous." Our engineering of humanity calls for someone who can remind us that we are not machines, algorithms, commodities, or brains, but human beings. Yang does this and more. He reminds us that a human being is a narrative. This book is written in very congruent ways to its content: It is a poetics of supervision that understands human beings, the supervisory process, and the relationships between teachers and students as stories. Supervision is not something that is automatically granted to who has tenure in the local agency; it requires an art of soul: the ability to tell and hear stories. When we forget that, and the ancient Taoist tradition from which it comes, when data-bytes of information displace stories, we will already be extinct as a species. This book is an antidote to that horror. Bravo!

Todd Dubose, PhD, Full Professor at The Chicago School of Professional Psychology

Lighting the Candle is a remarkable book, and only someone with an in-depth knowledge of Eastern and Western psychological wisdom could have written it—namely, Mark Yang. The five chapters combine case studies with a deep understanding of existential–humanistic psychology and its parallel—and the much earlier—writings of Lao Tzu and Zhuangzi. Such topics as psychotherapy, supervision, and client–therapist relationships take on fresh meaning when seen through the Eastern lens, as do the insights of Rollo May and Victor Frankl. Dr. Yang's translations are the work of a master poet, and his evocative accounts of clients and their struggles attest to his skill as a master therapist. *Lighting the Candle* is bound to become an instant classic.

Stanley Krippner, PhD, California Institute of Integral Studies

Central to the approach of existential–humanistic psychology are themes of the "big" questions in life: what it means to be human, how to make sense of evil, and the inevitability of death. Before psychology became a modern science, these questions were addressed in philosophy, religion, and the humanities. Mark Yang, in his new book, finds echoes of these questions in Taoist principles, as well as in Western mystical traditions. These questions, in existential–humanistic psychology as well as is ancient philosophies, are addressed most vividly through story. This book is full of such moving and enlightening stories—a wonderful teaching tool.

Ilene Serlin, PhD, Associated Distinguished Professor of Integral and Transpersonal Psychology, California Institute of Integral Studies

Lighting the Candle

Taoist Principles in Supervision Conducted from an Existential–Humanistic Perspective

Mark Yang, PsyD

Colorado Springs, CO
www.universityprofessorspress.com

Lighting the Candle: Taoist Principles in Supervision Conducted from an Existential–Humanistic Perspective

By Mark Yang

First Published in 2020, University Professors Press.

Print ISBN: 978-1-939686-65-7
ebook ISBN: 978-1-939686-66-4

University Professors Press
Colorado Springs, CO
www.universityprofessorspress.com

Front Cover Art by Myriam Zilles
Cover Design by Laura Ross

The portions of Kahlil Gibran's poems in chapters one and four are from the book *The Prophet* (2015). The book is now considered public domain so no permission is necessary for republication.

Zhuangzi's passages from the book *Wandering on the Way: Early Taoist Tales and Parables of Chuang Tzu* (V. Mair, Trans.) can be found in all five chapters of the book. Permission to reprint these passages has been granted by the University of Hawaii Press.

Table of Contents

Chapter 1	Introduction: The Beauty of Stories	1
Chapter 2	Humanistic Education: Lighting the Candle, Passing on the Flame	21
Chapter 3	Bruce's Story: An Encounter Through Song	41
Chapter 4	Tracy's Story: Steadiness in the Midst of Chaos	105
Chapter 5	Petrus' Story: Companionship in the Midst of Suffering	127

References 155
Index 161
About the Author 165

Chapter 1

Introduction: The Beauty of Stories

> Students are not receptacles to be crammed but candles to be lit.

> A true master according to the Eastern tradition embodies truth for the disciple and transmits it directly as a lit candle can light another. He represents the reality which is present, but as yet imperfectly released, in the disciple, and his purpose is to help the disciple to realize, in the Indian phrase, the eternal Guru and teacher in himself. When he has succeeded in doing this, the need of external Master and mediator is over. In short, the aim of the Master is to prove himself superfluous, since what he essentially is, the disciple is too (Fausset, 1969, p. 38).

Tales of Inspiration

This book is dedicated to all of the students I've met and have yet to meet throughout my travels in Asia delivering training in existential-humanistic psychology. Along the way, I've encountered numerous stories that uplift and inspire me. Each of these stories inspires me to remain in Asia to continue to promote existential-humanistic psychology and the way of the Tao. Human drama is best exemplified in stories—stories of pain, sacrifice, courage, inspiration, and beauty. An old Hasidic proverb observes: "Give people a fact or an idea and you enlighten their minds; give them a story and you touch their souls" (Alchemy, n.d.). The humanistic psychotherapist and writer Sheldon

Kopp (2013) shared another Hasidic tale regarding how God created human beings because he loved stories.

> There once was a great rabbi who would go into the forest to meditate, light a fire, say a special prayer for the people of Israel when misfortune threatened. His actions helped to avert the misfortune. The rabbi's disciple would similarly intercede on the behalf of the people. He too would go in the forest and offer the prayer but would admit to the Master of the Universe that he'd forgotten how to light the fire. Yet, the misfortune was also averted. Still later, another rabbi would also go in the forest and ask God to avert the misfortune even though he did not know how to light a fire nor say the prayer. But he'd beseech God by stating that he did know the place. And this was enough. Finally, it fell on Rabbi Israel of Rizhyn to help his people. He'd sit on his armchair, head in hand and implored God: "I am unable to light the fire and I do not know the prayer; I cannot even find the place in the forest All I can do is to tell the story, and this must be sufficient." And it was sufficient. (Kopp, 2013, p. 21)

Stories can be understood as personal myths, and as such they sustain us. Yet, so many of us are unfamiliar with our own myths. Too often when asked to share about ourselves, we tell of our achievements or acquisitions. Our personal myths, like hidden beams of a house that holds us together (May, 1991) are about who we are, not what we've done. Are we living for our resumes or our eulogies (Brooks, 2014)? Stories take time.[1] When we've stopped taking the time to listen to one another's stories, we seek out experts to do the listening and tell us how we should live. Another Hasidic teaching proclaims that whenever two Jews meet, if one has a problem, the other automatically becomes a rabbi (Kopp, 2013). A good psychotherapist is such a rabbi. She is a connoisseur of pain and beauty and a lover of music patiently listening to the themes and variations of the music in the client's story over and over again. She is also a nostalgia buff, never tiring of hearing about the good old days, and the bad old days (Storr, 1990). We are guests in our clients' lives and together with our supervisee sit at the feet of our

---

[1] For a more extensive reading on existential perspectives on Eastern and Western myths, please refer to the *Existential Psychology East–West* (Volume 1—Revised and Expanded Edition) and *Existential Psychology East–West* (Volume 2), also published by University Professors Press.

clients ready to learn, looking to be enchanted through the sharing of their stories!

Thus, this book is a compilation of Taoist parables, teaching stories in themselves, the life stories of students I've encountered along the way, and the stories that a few of my extraordinary supervisees have created together with their clients. Each of these stories about my students are deep encounters, and this book is dedicated to them because of all the ways they have enriched me through the sharing of their stories. And now I in turn share their stories with you with a decidedly Taoist twist.

The Perfect Bed and Breakfast

Taoists extol the wisdom to be found in darkness; thus, I will start with a story of failure and disappointment. One of the first things many psychology students have to endure in the first year of graduate school is a year's study of statistics and research methods, foundations of empiricism. Following methodologies derived from natural science, we are expected to operationalize—in other words, define the construct that we intend to study. It is with such a spirit that an earnest student, whom I will name "the seeker," relentlessly asked me to define existence. She began the inquiry by first asking if I was an existential therapist. I answered affirmatively, bracing myself for the question to follow, for I sensed that this was no simple inquiry. She then informed me that matters of existence had troubled her for a long time and asked expectantly for me to define existence for her, to her satisfaction. This was, of course, a reasonable request given that I identified myself as an existential psychologist. Yet I was stumped!

Sensing my struggle, several other students explained for me that existence cannot be defined and urged her to slow down and be patient to see what she might experience during the two-day workshop. However, the seeker became more agitated with each persuasion. Knowing that I could only slow things down so far, yet with no "brilliant" answer to satisfy the seeker's inquiry, I modestly informed her that I did not have such a definition for this is an impossible task. Hoping to satisfy her inquiry and thus reduce her agitation, I reminded her of the renowned opening lines of the Tao Te Ching, which stated that "The tao that can be told is not the eternal Tao. The name that can be named is not the eternal Name" (Lao Tzu, 1995). In addition, had I the time, I would have offered the seeker this beautiful prose describing the Tao, written by the English novelist Somerset Maugham (likely inspired by Verse 73 of the Tao Te Ching) in his book *The Painted Veil*:

> It is the Way and the Waygoer. It is the eternal road along which walk all beings, but no being made it, for itself is being. It is everything and nothing. From it all things spring, all things conform to it, and to it at last all things return. It is a square without angles, a sound which ears cannot hear, and an image without form. It is a vast net and though its meshes are as wide as the sea it lets nothing through. It is the sanctuary where all things find refuge. It is nowhere, but without looking out of the window you may see it. Desire not to desire, it reaches out and leaves all things to take their course. He that bends shall be made straight. Failure is the foundation of success and success is the lurking-place of failure; but who can tell when the turning point will come? He who strives after tenderness can become even as a little child. Gentleness brings victory to him who attacks and safety to him who defends. Mighty is he who conquers himself" (Maugham, 2004, p. 197)

Tao Te Ching, Verse 73 (excerpts)

Heaven's way does not strive
  Yet it always overcomes
It does not speak, yet it responds
It is not summoned, yet it appears
It does not hurry, yet it completes everything on time

The net of Heaven spans the universe
 Yet not the slightest thing ever slips by (Lao Tzi, 2003, p. 86)

No luck. My response served to increase the seeker's frustration for she persisted in her inquiry with even more intensity and not a little anger just below the surface. Desiring not to disappoint, informed by phenomenology, I went on to further explain that many of the most important things in life are subjective and cannot be objectively defined. The best we can do is to offer descriptions while acknowledging that true reality is, and will forever remain, both unknown and unknowable to us. I then followed up by asking her to define love, hoping that this would persuade the seeker to slow down and reflect upon her own experience.

By this point, many of the students (including myself) had become frustrated with this exchange and encouraged the seeker to once again stand down and wait. Seeing the futility of her request, the seeker retreated to her corner seat and sat sulking the rest of the day with no attempts to engage in any of the dialogue—a dark, brooding energy that permeated our small workshop. My disappointment was realized the next day when she chose not to return. Rationally, I knew that I did the best I could. Intuitively, I also knew that there were likely intrapersonal dynamics at play behind the intensity of her inquiry. Nevertheless, I could not shake off the mild failure and disappointment I felt for being unable to provide an adequate answer and be more helpful to this forceful seeker.

Yet within failure is the seed of wisdom, for two months later, another student of mine shared a very similar struggle with me when she was asked by a colleague to define existential psychology. The colleague was also an unrelenting seeker who would not let my student go until she gave an adequate definition. Exasperated, my student finally told the colleague that she would not be able to give a definition to his satisfaction. However, she shared with him what she loved about existential psychology and went on to give example after example of how existential psychology impacted her life. This succeeded in quieting the colleague, who later apologized to my student for his overbearing relentlessness.

My student's response enlightened me. It brought to my mind how matters of existence can only be experienced subjectively. Even though both seekers were looking for objective definitions, the answers they sought must be experienced subjectively. There is a subjective responsibility which they must own. I learned from my student that day that, paradoxically, it is likely the sharing of our own subjective experiences, not the objective definitions, will speak to the person most powerfully. Through his extensive work with encounter groups, Carl Rogers (1961) learned that "what is most personal is most general. If one can understand what is most real with one's own experience and unique for oneself at the deepest personal level of feeling and understanding, it is likely that it is the very element which would, if it were shared or expressed, speak most deeply to others" (p. 26). James Bugental (1999), who dedicated much of his writings and work to the importance of the subjective, understood this paradox very well. He wrote: "Yet there is a paradox here: Our commonalities are mostly objective, our individualities are principally subjective, and yet deeper in the subjective there resides a more subtle connectedness among all persons, perhaps even all life" (pp. 187–188). This must be what Lao Tzu and Somerset Maugham meant by the net that lets nothing through even though its meshes are as wide as the sea/universe.

I'm unlikely to meet that seeker again. However, the disappointment of not meeting her expectations became my impetus for teaching other seekers about the subjective–objective paradox of the nature of existence. Indeed, if I had the chance to come across that seeker or others like her, I'd offer a very different answer. Instead of trying to explain or teach, I'd offer the seeker my personal experience of existence. I'd share with her that the last glance shared between my dog and me prior to my departure for Asia over a decade and a half ago is what I'd understand as existence. For, ironically, it was at that moment of final separation that I felt existence most deeply. I'd go on to share with her that even though my dog was always there by my side, I felt her existence most intensely every time I'd pick her up from the vet. The look of helplessness she'd give me, asking how I could leave her in such a sterile cold place all day, would just melt my heart and help to reconnect with my love for her that was always present. That love was always present, but it was through vulnerability and pain that I came to a deeper connection with its existence. I'm not sure how the seeker would have responded to my subjective "definition." I'd like to think that perhaps my own subjectivity would have connected with whatever pain was behind her seeking. But I'll never know. What I do know is that her relentless questioning caused me pain. But it also helped me to gain a deeper understanding and accumulate more knowledge to share with others in regard to the definition or meaning of existence.

While the seeker was not able to benefit from my subjective sharing, Max, Margaret's husband and the co-owner of the Perfect Bookstore,[2] was able to resonate deeply with the essence of the above story. The Perfect Bookstore was the setting for the workshop where this story took place. Providentially, I was able to share my new "definition" of existence at a later workshop conducted back at the Perfect Bookstore. As we went around the room sharing about how we'd each define existence subjectively, Max shared that such a moment was clear in his mind. He shared how deeply present and connected to existence he felt during a spring afternoon prior to the opening of the bookstore. The air was crisp and all the windows were opened. He was alone at the bookstore contentedly assembling one wooden bookshelf after another. The moment was deeply meaningful for him for a number of reasons.

---

[2] The Story of the Perfect Bookstore can be found in Chapter 3 of this book.

The bookstore represented the pursuit of his wife's dream, which he delightedly partook of. It represented a sort of freedom that was not commonly pursued among his peers. It also reawakened a love for woodworking that he had left behind because of the "realities" of everyday living. His sharing was poignant, authentic, and rippled on, since I would share his moment with students during numerous subsequent workshops.

But the story did not end there for the Perfect Bookstore turned into the perfect bed and breakfast! A year later Margaret's husband shared with me that he had decided to quit his job and start a B&B so that he could reengage with woodworking and pursue his own dream. Wow! I was simultaneously flabbergasted, inspired, and filled with anxiety. "Are you sure?" I asked him. He assured me that this was not an impulsive decision for he was well aware of the commitment and had made careful preparations financially. Max was the envy of his colleagues and yet, at the same time, he could also sense their discomfort at witnessing Max living in such a risky manner. This is an ongoing story. Max and Margaret dared to take seriously the responsibility of being the authors of their own lives. They are consummating their existence. At the time of this writing, they have sold their perfect bookstore, another form of letting go, and are operating the Perfect B&B. For together they recognize that existence cannot be postponed!

It is such stories of courage that inspire me to choose to remain in Asia and breathe the polluted air in Beijing. Yet Max, Margaret, and I are not alone. Many others are also living courageous lives of freedom in pursuit of meaning. Victor Frankl (1985, 1988) passionately defended *The Will to Meaning* and *Man's Search for Meaning* (titles of two of his books) thusly: He argued that the most valid proof for the existence of water is the instinct for thirst. For it is inconceivable that nature would create thirst unless there was the existence of water. Similarly, one's will for meaning can be compared to the essential instinct for thirst. As you read on, you'll discover how indomitable our will to meaning can be. After witnessing these stories, how can I not remain in Asia to participate in this drama, partake in its creative nourishment, and share their inspiration with you throughout this book? Let's continue with the story of Daisy, followed by a tale of a liberating dream across time.

Awakened to Prada

Daisy had been thinking for a while about leaving her job as a headhunter and becoming a full-time therapist. She shared a story of entering the office of an accomplished female executive who was making a very comfortable living. She made more money than she had time to spend. After Daisy was ushered into the plush office, the executive was excited to show the contents of her file cabinets. Anticipating the tools of the executive's craft, Daisy expected to see volumes and volumes of books or top-secret files. Instead, a vault of expensive high-end fashion shoes was revealed to Daisy. The executive lamented her work and said to Daisy, "Why would I store artifacts of my work here when I can be surrounded by the beautiful things that I truly love?" Daisy was shocked and found herself pitying this trapped executive. The executive was immensely successful but equally unhappy. In a parallel fashion, Daisy saw the emptiness of her current pursuit as a successful headhunter. She vowed to herself that she would never allow herself to become like this executive.

During the same year, Daisy's grandmother also passed away. Her grandmother was a paragon of self-sacrifice. The grandmother did not allow herself to live for herself. Daisy was appreciative of her grandmother but also felt very sad for a life unlived. Daisy told herself that she must not forget herself in the midst of serving others.

Finally, Daisy resolved to take an intervening step and backpacked through India on her own. Daisy spoke fluent English but not all of the people that she encountered in India did. Daisy discovered that many of the things that she "needed" to live were illusions and found that she could truly wander and be self-sufficient based on very little materially and psychologically. Daisy then came upon a shaman, who divined, "You are ready to embark upon what you were hoping to do." This was her final confirmation.

Daisy returned to China after her trip and promptly tendered her resignation. She is now earning one-tenth of her previous salary and living the simple life. She rediscovered the joy of simplicity. The final beautiful piece of the puzzle was that Daisy, being a successful and accomplished woman, had dated frequently but never found Mr. Right. She came to the workshop six months pregnant with her first child!

The Birdsong of Existence

Though I have never met him in person, James Bugental, the eminent American existential–humanistic psychotherapist, has been a supervisor to me through his writings and his training videos. Continuing his lineage here in Asia, I often encourage my students to listen to the music rather than the lyrics when conducting therapy. Bugental (1999) had a nice way of putting it by teaching us to facilitate therapy such that it encourages our clients to "talk *out of* themselves rather than *about* themselves." This meant that often in therapy what mattered most was not what was said but *how* it was said. Eugene Gendlin (as cited in Bugental 1999), the founder of focusing, taught the same concept. He presented research that found even undergraduate students with little to no training can recognize effective versus non-effective sessions based upon listening to how clients expressed themselves. This is easy to recognize but difficult to facilitate.

A beautiful piece of art that helps me to illustrate the principle of listening to the music rather than the lyrics comes from the movie *The Shawshank Redemption.* I am told that *The Shawshank Redemption* is on the top-ten list of many movie fans in China! I believe the reason that this movie has such a wide appeal across cultures is because of the existential themes that are dramatized in the movie. These themes are universal and resonate across cultures. That is why I have used this classic movie in numerous workshops in Asia to illustrate the concept of freedom from an existential perspective.

It was after one such workshop that a young lady shared her beautiful dream with me. I will detail her dream after presenting its context that arose out of, in my opinion, one of the most beautiful moments in cinematic history filled with profound symbolism. If you've watched the movie, you'll know which moment I'm talking about when it comes to "listening to the music." I use this scene to teach my supervisees that therapy and life are about creating and being attuned to such ephemeral and transformative moments. Yes, there are predictable stages in the therapeutic process. But what I find to matter most in therapy is not the progression across these broad stages but the fundamental shifts in consciousness, perspective, and attitude that occur as the result of these beautiful transformative moments of connection. It is critically important that we become attuned to such melodies and opportunities in life. That we become attuned to moments for creation, rebellion, and seize upon them to create life-changing beauty. If we are overly focused upon our preconceived plans, or looking for consecutive stages to traverse, we will more than likely miss these important opportunities for creation.

Altogether, these moments are less than one percent of the total time spent in therapy, but it is during these ephemeral yet eternal one percent moments that transformation occurs. The other ninety-nine percent are not without their importance. We need our treatment plans for they help us to organize our thinking and manage our own anxieties. How will seeds flourish if we do not laboriously till the soil? After all, it "only" took Andy, the main character in the movie, six years of weekly letters to the bureaucrats for the library to be built. He had a vision and the perseverance to stick to it. The library, along with Andy's other meaningful life projects, would not have been built without a plan of action and the determination to carry it through.

Nevertheless, Andy was also free and flexible enough to recognize and seize this beautiful moment of creation before it passed him by. Andy did not wake up that day thinking he would liberate the prisoners within Shawshank Prison. He did not even know that he was to receive his library reward that day after six years of faithful and persistent letter writing. It was impossible for Andy to predict or plan for such moments. Yet paradoxically, Andy had been preparing all of his life for such a moment. His knowledge of opera, literature, and the arts was likely the result of life-long cultivation. In addition, the courage for rebellion was born out of the regular abuse and earlier beatings he endured as a prisoner. This includes the bemused disrespect he received from his jailers immediately following the triumphant celebration of his arduous accomplishment as the result of his library letter campaign. Andy was able to maintain his dignity and channel his anger through this meaningful act of creation and rebellion.

But back to the music and the beautiful narration of Red, played by Morgan Freeman:

> I have no idea to this day what them two Italian ladies were singin' about. Truth is, I don't want to know. Some things are best left unsaid. I like to think they were singin' about something so beautiful it can't be expressed in words, and makes your heart ache because of it.
>
> I tell you, those voices soared. Higher and farther than anybody in a gray place dares to dream. It was like some beautiful bird flapped into our drab little cage and made these walls dissolve away...and for the briefest of moments—every last man at Shawshank felt free. (Glotzer & Darabont, 1994)

I believe Red was speaking for all of us. He was talking about music and the love of life, but he could just as easily have been describing the process of therapy. It is remarkable to me that though Red did not understand the lyrics of the opera, he fully understood that it was beautiful, and it moved his soul. The lyrics were not important. He did not want to know. But Red knew that they were singing about something so beautiful that "it cannot be expressed with words and makes our hearts ache because of it." Though Red was not familiar with opera, he knew beauty and how both fleeting and eternal it can be. Red knew that "The bird does not sing because it knows the answer. It sings because it has a song. And the song is existence" (quote offered by my colleague Erik Craig at the closing of the Second Annual International Conference on Existential Psychology at Shanghai China, May 2012).

Back to the dream of the young lady in China. I've had occasion to share the beauty of Red's words and explicate the existential themes found within *The Shawshank Redemption* with numerous workshop participants throughout China. The examination of the existential themes in the movie helped us to appreciate the depths in this beautiful story of inspiration. However, what I did not expect was for this moment of inspiration to extend for over a period of one year. I showed *The Shawshank Redemption* to workshop participants in Shanghai in May of 2012, immediately prior to the Second Annual International Conference on Existential Psychology. Yet, it was not until June of 2013 when I returned to Shanghai for another workshop that I discovered how meaningful and impactful the movie was. One young lady waited an entire year to share the following dream with me:

> I dreamed that I was in a paper labyrinth chased by an assailant. Amid the chase, I was fortunate to find a large chest that offered concealment from my pursuer. I climbed into the chest and eventually found that I was not alone! To my amazement, I found another man in the chest with me and he desired to kiss me! I was now caught between a rock and a hard place. The chest offered protection from the assailant but the man in the chest wanted to kiss me. What was I to do?
>
> It was at this moment of feeling incredibly trapped that the operatic moment in *The Shawshank Redemption* came back to me. I heard a voice permitting and urging me to listen to the music, even though I had no understanding of the words. The voice urged me to allow myself to be carried away from the

walls of social convention. I knew the voice was permitting and encouraging me to follow the desires of my heart and kiss this man if I so desired. I am free!

It was a moment of liberation shared across the Pacific, from East to West, over the period of a year. The lady shared that at the time of the initial workshop, she discovered that her first boyfriend had married someone else. This brought up painful memories of their breakup, along with her fears of being left behind and unwanted in a society that would have women married before the age of 30. Yet, the lady shared that Red's words from the movie resonated in her heart: "You do not need to understand the music. The important thing is that you're free to follow the music and the desires of your heart. You're free to move on and let go of the walls of the social conventions of the past."

I was stunned and incredibly honored to receive this unexpected gift across time. I could not believe that she waited one year to share this transformative moment with me. She held onto this moment for all this time anticipating our next meeting to offer and share her gratitude. These ephemeral moments are eternal! I was simply sharing some existential themes that further accentuated the beauty and tragedy of life, projected upon the movie screen. Little did I expect to find myself rewarded with the honor of participating in the liberation of a lady who awakened to her soul in the midst of her pain and loss. How blessed and fortunate am I!

Three Cups of Coffee

Not being a coffee drinker, I nevertheless went on a quest for a good cup of coffee in Malaysia with my friend and fellow existentialist Zheng Liren because of his deep passion for everything related to coffee. Liren makes a point of visiting specialty coffee shops wherever he travels. He told me about how to roast beans, and how to go about brewing and tasting a good cup of coffee. As he talked, I was reminded of how existentialists are like baristas, sommeliers, and tea aficionados in that we are all connoisseurs of bitterness. Liren definitely qualifies for being a connoisseur of that bittersweet liquid. He educated us about the finer points of bitterness. He taught me the language of the barista. I never knew that coffee could be sour and full-bodied. Tasting is Believing! For all this, Liren's reward was me showing up with a cup of coffee from McDonald's filled with cream and sugar. No good act goes unpunished!

Anyway, on a previous trip to Malaysia, Liren found a specialty coffee shop named Coffee Famille in Kuala Lumpur, and he promised to take Evone, another existentialist, and I along to revisit the shop and its owner named Ving. Liren also promised to brew his own cup of coffee with Ving's permission. We arrived on a quiet Thursday evening and were granted Ving's undivided attention. Liren went ahead and brewed his own cup of coffee, telling us about how a temperature difference of a few degrees would result in a different taste! He also demonstrated the patience required to achieve even pouring lest you over-brew one section of the beans in the filter. Such precision! I was in the presence of a connoisseur who took his art seriously!

As we sat down to enjoy our cups of lovingly brewed coffee, we invited Ving to join us to share her story about the opening of the coffee shop. Ving showed little hesitance as she recounted how she fell in love with coffee in her teenage years. She went on to tell us that she learned to become a barista at a specialty coffee shop during her university studies. Naturally, I assumed that becoming a barista in Taiwan was a nice second degree she received from Taiwan. Ving looked puzzled look and corrected me by telling me that she specifically went to Taiwan to pursue training as a barista. The university degree was the means, with her apprenticeship at a specialty coffee shop being the end. Her goal all along was to return to Malaysia and open a coffee shop of her own. Such dedication and clarity of purpose at a relatively young age!

Yet, dreams are rarely realized without obstacles. Ving's brother and mother were both strongly opposed to her decision to open a coffee shop. Part of the reason for their opposition was her business plan. Ving wanted to preserve the ambiance of the coffee shops that she experienced in Taiwan. Despite a higher volume of foot traffic, Ving did not want to open up her shop in a mall. "Malls are not conducive for sitting down to enjoy a cup of good coffee." A good cup of coffee requires time, and each cup of coffee must be individually brewed. The process cannot be rushed. Nothing standardized and manualized. All of this ran counter to the anonymity and standardized efficiency that characterize most of the coffee shops found in shopping malls.

Furthermore, Ving's brother was an accountant, and he was appalled to learn that Ving had no desire to expand her business. In fact, as Ving looked around her shop, she said that if she were to change or move, she'd move to a smaller shop to attempt to preserve the ambience that she wanted to achieve. The beautiful thing, of course, is that even though her brother was opposed to her business plan, he gave Ving the start-up capital she needed to start the shop. Action speaks louder than words. I believe Ving's brother invested because he could see her unshakable passion and that such passion must not be quenched.

I visited Ving's coffee shop during a five-day introductory workshop I was giving on existential psychology. I could not help but reflect on how Ving's approach to coffee and business parallels the existential approach to supervision and therapy. What Ving knew inherently in her soul was that there is also a soul and essence to coffee that must not be institutionalized and thus demolished. Each region produces its own flavor of coffee, and there are numerous coffee regions in the world. Typically, one only gets to sample coffee from a few regions in a franchised coffee shop. The specialty coffee shop owner knows intimately the coffees that he or she serves on her menu. Ving develops a close relationship with that coffee bean. Many roast their own beans, fresh, once a week so it will not become stale and lose its flavor. And, of course, the beans must be ground fresh for each cup. Furthermore, there are various ways of brewing to achieve different tastes. It is anything but standardized and manualized. Like a good therapist, the true barista strives to bring the best out of each set of beans, and each cup of coffee is one step along that process. Ving makes sacrifices to preserve the soul of the coffee that she brews and serves just as therapists and clients must together strive to preserve the soul and essence of each of our clients lest their voice and individuality get drowned out in the cacophony of the masses. Similarly, a good supervisor must tailor her supervision to the needs of each of her supervisees. There are no standardized methods to supervision. Each supervisee has their own soul, their own particular strengths and weaknesses. For supervision to be effective, it is a matter of mutual adaption.

Finally, Ving shared the struggles she experienced and the grace that she's received in the process of pursuing her dream. An idealistic business plan will be severely challenged by the realities of the world. Ving admitted to challenging financial struggles. She is the major shareholder with two other partners. Ving also employs a full-time helper named Lawrence who is quite a baker in his own right. Several times in the nascent life of her dream, Ving ran into problems with cash flow. Anyone who has started their own business knows that such problems are ubiquitous. Ving shared with emotion how difficult those times were for her. She's had to admit to her detractors that her plans were indeed flawed—the painful discovery of the limits and the possible end of her dreams. Yet, Ving also shared that it was during such times that the miraculous took place. It was during both of these nadirs that Ving received financial help from the unlikeliest of sources: Her customers! One customer was an admirer of Ving's clarity of purpose, tenacity, and courage in daring to pursue her dream. Thus, he simply made an unsolicited interest-free loan to Ving with a two-year monthly repayment plan. In the other instance, another admirer decided to make a capital injection in exchange for part-ownership because Ving was living the dream that she was unable or unwilling to live. Through witnessing her emotion, one can tell that these unsolicited acts of trust were overwhelming for the struggling Ving. They were completely unexpected and demonstrate the power of acceptance and unconditional positive regard. It is extraordinary to live under such grace. Liren, Evone, and I were all deeply moved as we listened to Ving recount her beautiful story of survival and struggle. Of course, this story was shared over three very meaningfully brewed cups of coffee. There was such beauty to Ving's courage and pain. Her coffee shop is a living inspiration to the three of us. This was my first and, thankfully, not the last encounter with Ving. I was able to return to Malaysia on numerous other occasions for training and continue to journey with Ving in her development. As I bore witness to Ving's journey of growth, I was able to chronicle such growth, the fruits of which are scattered throughout the following chapters of this book. As you'll see, the story of Ving's journey is a significant source of inspiration for me, one that I feel fortunate to be able to share with you.

A Life-Long Apprentice

Finally, I offer you the story of my own development as an existential psychotherapist. My dream was not to become a psychologist. I always wanted to become a pilot when I grew up. So what did I do? I enrolled in college and declared computer engineering as my major. Go figure! I did not know who I was or what I wanted to become. I decided to study computer engineering because I enjoyed computers and did not have the grades to become an aeronautical engineer, the closest thing to a pilot that I can think of. Computer engineering felt like a good compromise. Most important, I needed security and opted for the safe choice of computer engineering as the next step toward my family's pursuit of the Chinese-American dream. My path was set and I was safely on my way . . . except . . . I was a lousy engineer! Though I did well in mathematics in high school, I reached my limit in college. It was painful and humbling to come up against my limits. I was forced to admit to myself that others were better at engineering and mathematics. So, reluctantly, I switched my major to psychology and became a psychologist because I was a failed engineer. I am a Plan B psychologist and thank God for it for I know I'm not alone in this regard.

The decision to get off the safe and well-worn path was painful and filled with fear. One of the things that I enjoyed about studying computer engineering was that I was in a "tracked major." Just about all of my courses were laid out, and all I had to do was to put my nose to the grindstone and walk that safe path one track at a time. Eventually, I would arrive at the promised land. I looked down upon those who were not "on the path" and had to deal with the confusion and anxiety of selecting classes every semester. How I pitied their struggle for their indeterminate existence. Of course, I did not dare to lift my nose from that grindstone and contemplate my indeterminate existence. However, with my failure as a computer engineer, I became a commoner, one of the ambiguous souls that were the target of my pity. My future became uncertain—my first major encounter with freedom, from an existential perspective. What should I study? How did I get to the promised land now that I was not good enough to traverse the gilded traditional path? I was curious about psychology but it was certainly not the promised land. I was lost and troubled. So I sought counsel.

The first "wise man" I sought out was Dr. Michael Tanner, the director of my computer engineering program. He'd been to the promised land. He worked for IBM and looked like he had the right stuff. Surely he would have good advice for me. He learned of my interest in psychology and suggested the field of artificial intelligence, which combined my interest in computers and psychology, a rational choice that made a lot of sense. But something was missing. So I went to the second "wise man," who turned out to be an academic counselor in the department of psychology. Still thinking like an engineer, I was logical and systematic in seeking my counsel. The "counselor" was true to his name and task for he advised me on the courses that I needed to take in psychology were I to change majors and graduate on time. He did his job as an "academic counselor" but, unfortunately, was effective in persuading me away from psychology for he failed to intuit my need. Psychology felt dry and uninspiring as embodied by this representative.

Desperate and directionless, I ventured into the office of Dr. Ralph Quinn, the hippy professor who taught Introduction to Humanistic Psychology, my first college-level course in psychology. Sadly, his course was the only formal course in humanistic psychology that was available in both my undergraduate and graduate program. Ralph, who preferred all his students call him by his first name, did not offer any advice or suggestions that day. All he did was care for me by listening intently to my pain and struggles. I'm able to describe to you now the wisdom of his companionship because of my subsequent studies in existential–humanistic psychology. At that time, as a lost 20-year-old, I had no idea what took place during the appointment but it felt right. I remember walking out of his office in a comfortable daze, a daze that I understand now as a shift in consciousness. Unwittingly, I experienced companionship and faith. He offered me no explanations but the experience of being heard and trusted. Nothing was solved for I still did not know if psychology was the right choice for me. I would not know for a long time. But Ralph's companionship helped me to experience that unknowing was okay. I did not have to figure it all out then. Important things took time. He did not tell me these things directly. He embodied them for me instead. He did not tell me about psychology, he helped me to experience it in the present moment. So even though I did not walk out of his office with a clear, rational sense of what I was to do with one of the most important decisions in my life, intuitively, my body, spirit, and soul came to realize that the experience I had just encountered was what I was after. I eventually chose to pursue psychology wholeheartedly and left artificial intelligence, a compromise, and computer information sciences, a derivative of the original secure path, behind.

That single conversation changed my life though I certainly did not know it at the time. Fast forward 25 years later, and I once again visited my old college campus but was unable to get in touch with Ralph. However, I found out how fortunate I was for I heard of similar stories of impact from several colleagues who attended the same workshop that week. I was one of Ralph's first students. He was a first-year professor at the time that I first sought out his counsel. He was far from perfect for he had begun his second career as a middle-aged single father with a buttload of debt! Yet, he was perfect for me and for many others since. What I learned was that for 25 years and counting, Ralph humbly committed himself to his teaching at the local university. He gained no notoriety nor fame. Yet his work ripples on through myself and numerous others he's touched. Anonymously, he's impacted a number of us at critical developmental junctures of our lives. Through his example and companionship, he mentored us through critical times of uncertainty and helped us to have the faith to find ourselves in our own life journeys. His spirit ripples on through the words of this page, and his impact upon my life is poetically expressed through the poem at the end of this chapter.

I believe Ralph was a Taoist after Zhuangzi's heart for he, too, chose to drag his tail in the mud, laboring in the backwaters of a small psychology department at the University of California, Santa Cruz. He sought neither fame nor veneration. He was just an ordinary professor. Yet coming back 25 years later to find Ralph persisting in living out his calling, I gained a deeper appreciation for Zhuangzi's (2006) parable of a tortoise dragging its tail in the mud:

> Chuang Tzu was one day fishing in the Pu river when the King of Chu dispatched two senior officials to visit him with a message. The message said, "I would like to trouble you to administer my lands."
>
> Chuang Tzu kept a firm grip on his fishing rod and said, "I hear that in Chu there is a sacred tortoise which died three thousand years ago. The King keeps this in his ancestral temple, wrapped and enclosed. Tell me, would this tortoise have wanted to die and leave his shell to be venerated? Or would he rather have lived and continued to crawl about in the mud?"
>
> The two senior officials said, "It would rather have lived and continued to crawl about in the mud."
>
> Chuang Tzu said, "Shove off, then! I will continue to crawl about in the mud! (Chapter 17, para. 35)

Even though I eventually decided to switch majors and traverse down a less secure path that is psychology, the time of uncertainty was far from over for, at the time of graduation, I once again faced uncertainty. Many of my friends were looking forward to graduation and entering the workforce or ministry, other paths that were also well traversed. The choice facing me was whether to continue my studies in psychology. I knew that an advanced degree was necessary if I wanted to make a career in psychology, but the prospect of another four or five years of studies was daunting to me. Did I really want to engage in four or five years of additional studies after just completing four years of university? Furthermore, one year of graduate school tuition equaled four years of undergraduate fees! Most of my friends thought that I was masochistic for considering additional studies. I was once again torn. So I returned to Ralph for counsel.

This time around was different. I encountered a thoughtful shifu (master) who offered his opinion that if it were up to him, the study of psychology would take on an apprentice model where the apprentice would learn the trade from his/her shifu through living together. Ralph taught me to respect our field and that becoming a good therapist is a life-long pursuit. So, of course, one should invest at least four to five years to earn an advanced degree. Curiously, inspiration replaced intimidation. Once again, I knew in my bones that Ralph was right. I made the decision to walk the road less traveled and took my chances in applying for graduate school. One step at a time, I told myself. See if you can get in first before worrying about how to pay for it. I am thankful for the wisdom that I had then for if I had taken on the entire mountain, I would never have begun the journey. As Lao Tzu famously reminded us in verse 64 of the Tao Te Ching, "A tree that fills a man's embrace grows from a seedling. A tower nine stories high starts with one brick. A journey of a thousand miles begins with a single step" (Lao Tzu, 2003, p. 77).

Fast-forward four years and you would find me taking a walk with my mentor from graduate school. Dr. Winston Gooden was a popular professor so many competed for his time. Thus, inviting him out for walks was my way to ensure time with him. During our last walk before leaving for my final year of internship, Winston shared with me that he recently read somewhere that seasoned clinicians were ten years in the making after graduation! I became exasperated upon hearing this and shared with him Ralph's counsel. I also shared my exasperation in learning that, paradoxically, the period of professional growth becomes lengthier the higher one climbs! I pressed on and asked him what's to be said ten years after graduation? Winston simply laughed at me and said, "Your clients will offer you a simple thank-you." There was no denying that Winston was speaking the truth.

It is now 25 years since that walk with Winston, and I am on the other side of the mentoring relationship. I find myself sharing with my own doctoral students that the four years they've invested in obtaining their doctorate is only an introduction to clinical psychology. For how much can you learn about psychodynamic, CBT, family systems, or humanistic psychology in a 40-hour class? I know that my students understand this intellectually just as I did. Yet, I can also imagine them thinking, "I spent all that money and time on just an introduction! Oh My God!"

Yet truth passes the test of time. I also have the honor of meeting together with graduates as they share with me now how they better understand what I meant. They find that there is so much to learn and too little time. Now, like Winston and Ralph, I'm the one who is smiling and nodding, and this brings me great satisfaction. Ralph was the first among several mentors who helped me to become who I am today. That rippling process continues for now I, too, am a mentor for others who need guidance and companionship in their journeys toward authenticity and professional growth. This is one of the main purposes of the book: to offer gratitude to my mentors and pass along their wisdom to those I'm fortunate to be able to teach and supervise in my own journey. It's about lighting the candle and passing on the flame. Having graduated from Ralph and Winston's formal mentorship, I've been fortunate to come under the guidance of Dave Elkins, who taught me about the importance of authenticity and wrote the chapter about tortoises dragging their tails in the mud in my other book, *Existential Psychology and the Way of the Tao* (Yang, 2017). Dave is a poet at heart and wrote a touching poetic tribute to his wise therapist and mentor titled "My Old Jungian Therapist."[3] He wrote of how this wise 73-year-old man had the patience to be lost with him as he struggled in his own dark labyrinthine path, offering him nothing but his faith that took a lifetime to build. That therapy, like my own encounter with Ralph, ripples on through the remainder of his life. Dave's tribute reminds me that there are many tortoises dragging their tails in the mud as they live out their authentic existence.

I hope that the rest of this book will serve as a good introduction to the ways of the Tao and help you to live out your authentic existence in the course of practicing existential psychotherapy. I'm not sure what you will take away from the story of my journey of learning. Will you be daunted, inspired, or perhaps both? My goal in sharing my journey with you is to let you know that I, too, am on my journey and that we are fellow travelers. Let us delight in the journey and not the destination for to travel well is better than to arrive.

---

[3] Elkins, D. N. (1997). My old Jungian analyst (poem). *Journal of Humanistic Psychology, 38(1),* 41.

Chapter 2

Humanistic Education: Lighting the Candle, Passing on the Flame

What is our role as supervisors? Are we instructors, teachers, gurus, parents, mentors, role models, or expert technicians? Perhaps all of the above. Conventionally, supervision is conceived as the teaching of clinical skills. Certainly, this is an important element of supervision. Supervision frequently involves case conceptualization, an advanced skill often taught in place of micro-skills. The analogy that I like to employ is that we need to teach and model for our supervisees the basics of driving before introducing navigational skills. For often if our supervisees are able to drive smoothly, the direction that their therapy takes will naturally become clearer. And from the humanistic perspective, that direction is co-constituted. The therapist's role is to be a guide by the side and not a sage on the stage as we facilitate our client's journey in the exploration of their inner terrains.

However, in line with the existential–humanistic approach, we must ask: Is there more? What else is there to supervision beyond case formulation, the teaching of clinical skills, and the development of a competent therapist? What is the end goal of supervision? How about awakening the soul of the trainee? Helping the supervisee to become a whole person so that they, too, can help their clients along that same journey. Brene Brown (2010), defined courage (the Latin root of the word courage is *cor*, which means heart) as the telling of one's story of who one is with one's whole heart. Wholehearted people are those who have the courage to be imperfect. How do we help our supervisees to become not only competent but wholehearted therapists?

What are our responsibilities as supervisors? When it comes to competence in traditional supervision, we typically help our supervisees develop the necessary technical or clinical skills to practice psychotherapy. Yet, skills training is only the beginning. As they mature, supervisees (and supervisors) must come to learn that there are no advanced skills, only advanced movement, and that life is about refinement, not perfection. And farther along that developmental path, some may even trade mastery for mystery. Again, there is much more to supervision than skills and much more to life than mastery. If we focus solely on skills training, we risk leaving our supervisees unbalanced. Typical of most supervisors in educational institutions in psychology today, we fall into the trap of developing our supervisee's intellect while neglecting their souls. Sadly, many recognize the body only as that which carries the head/brain while missing out on the deep wisdom that the body itself holds. Knowledge and skills are about the intellect. while clinical wisdom involves the integration of the intellect with heart/soul.

Rachel Naomi Remen (n.d.), best-selling author and professor of integrative medicine at the University of California San Francisco, recognized the same imbalance when she started the Institute for the Study of Health and Illness[1] as a response to the "deformative power of medical training." She developed programs and curricula at the institute to enable students to embody the deep values that inspired them to enter into medicine as a profession in the first place. Dr. Remen recognizes that the tools of healing involve "skills" such as presence, listening, and touch and strives to pass on such wisdom to doctors in training. These elements were not part of her training as a physician. Back then, she was taught that knowledge and information were key and that as a physician what was most important was what she knew. However, as she gained experience and wisdom in the art of healing, she discovered that she did not need to be in the know most of the time. Instead, if she were able to listen attentively to her patients, to their essential selves, to their souls, they often would sense the direction of their own healing and wholeness. Therefore, Dr. Remen let go of her theories about people. She discontinued her diagnoses and agendas. She would, more often than not, sit together with her patients, wait, and listen for their hidden beauty within. Their place of beauty is often the place of their greatest integrity. In her own words:

> As a counselor to people with cancer, I used to be ashamed of not being able to provide a more cognitive framework for what I do or offer a theoretical rationale for why I say what I say. I no longer feel this way. I also used to believe that things that could be expressed in numbers were truer than things that could only

[1] http://www.rishiprograms.org/about-2/

> be said in words. I no longer believe that either. It has been my experience that presence is a more powerful catalyst for change than analysis and that we can know beyond doubt things we can never understand.
>
> In some mysterious way, the life in someone may even use us to strengthen itself. Many years ago when I prepared for the final session with every patient, I used to review in my mind the milestones and turning points in our work together that had led to their healing. I would come up with a list of these in which I played a rather central role. Carefully I would go through my notes and document the thoughtful intervention I had made back in March or the powerful interpretation I had offered last September. But when I asked the people themselves to talk about their own experience of healing, they would rarely come up with more than half of my list. The rest of the time, they would share things that surprised me, chance remarks and facial expressions that they had interpreted in ways that evoked in them some profound and liberating insight. Then they would give me example after example of how they were able to use this insight to change their lives. Nodding sagely, I would have no recollection of the event at all.
>
> Clearly, I had been used to delivering a message of healing to them that did not originate in me. This has happened so often that I have become accustomed to it. It can be a little hard on the ego, but only at first. (Remen, 2000, pp. 90–91).

Irvin Yalom and Ginny Elkin (1974) wrote of the same phenomena in the book *Everyday Gets a Little Closer: A Twice-Told Therapy.* Yalom was courageous and creative enough to design a therapy for Ginny, who was struggling with writer's block. His ingenious project was to ask Ginny to write about her experience in therapy, and Yalom would do the same. Yalom was always interested in writing, and this was also a way for him to develop his skills as a writer. Yalom and Ginny would each write their reflections about their sessions immediately after the session and then place them in sealed envelopes to be handed to Yalom's secretary. The secretary would hold onto the envelopes and then distribute them to the other person every few months. This proved to be extremely educational for Yalom. He was astonished to find that Ginny recalled few of his brilliant interpretations, knowledge, and "wisdom" that were years in the making. Of course, these interpretations were what Yalom valued for they reflected his brilliance and control, the tangible proof of the effectiveness of therapy. Yet, Ginny did not recall many of these brilliant interpretations. Effectiveness and "true wisdom," Yalom learned, involved matters of the heart. What Ginny valued was Yalom's genuine caring, evidenced by such matters as that he noticed she changed her hairstyle, the little details that he remembered about their conversations. Details and actions about which Yalom had absolutely no recall! How are we to conduct therapy then, Yalom mused?

These experiences taught Yalom that he needed to reconstruct his early conception of the factors that led to healing. It was not that the insights and interpretations he had of the client were unhelpful. But what he was mistaken about is how they helped. Ginny's improvement was not so much the result of Yalom's penetrating insights. What healed was the experience of being seen, being heard, and being loved. Our expert theories and knowledge have their place, for they help us to keep our interest in the client while the real agent of change, the relationship and our deep caring, work their magic. And it's precisely such interest that the client values over and above the intellectual explanations we offer, backed by our theory.

Therefore, in order to develop competent therapists of the heart, if we are to teach our supervisees about embodiment and being wholehearted, we must recognize that our goals as supervisors are not only to impart specialized expert training but also the awakening of the charismatic, heroic, and magical qualities within each supervisee. We must recognize that students are not vessels to be filled but candles to be lit. For Carl Jung understood that "the sole purpose of human existence is to kindle a light of meaning in this darkness of mere being" (as cited in Spinelli, 2005, p. 202). Consider the words from Hugh l'Anson Fausset (1969) in his book, *The Flame and the Light*:

> A true master according to the Eastern tradition embodies truth for the disciple and transmits it directly as a lit candle can light another. He represents the reality which is present, but as yet imperfectly released, in the disciple, and his purpose is to help the disciple to realize, in the Indian phrase, the eternal Guru and teacher in himself. When he has succeeded in doing this, the need of external Master and mediator is over. In short, the aim of the Master is to prove himself superfluous, since what he essentially is, the disciple is too. (p. 38)

We must understand that "true teachers use themselves as bridges over which they invite their students to cross; then, having facilitated their crossing, joyfully collapse, encouraging them to create bridges of their own" (Kazantzakis, N., n.d.). And "A great teacher never strives to explain her vision; she simply invites you to stand beside her and see for yourself" (Inman, 2009). Alexandra Trenfor (2014) concurs, "The best teachers are those who show you where to look, but don't tell you what to see." Indeed we can lead a horse to water but we cannot make it drink. Similarly, we can lead people to knowledge but cannot make them think. Nevertheless, we can inspire! A good supervisor not only instructs, she can also inspire! Good supervision is as much about inspiration as it is about information.

Taking this even further, when dealing with existential themes, often there are no solutions to be offered or interventions to be taught. As illustrated through Petrus' story in Chapter 5 on Companionship in the Midst of Suffering, the best that we can offer as supervisors sometimes is the willingness to get lost together and demonstrate that getting lost is not a failure but part of the learning and healing process. This brings to mind the wisdom of the Hasidic sages who join pilgrims in their search rather than offering them authoritarian teachings. One such sage described his leadership by likening his pilgrims to a band of wanderers who have become lost in a deep, dark forest. They chance upon their guru, who has been lost even longer. Unaware of his helplessness, they ask him to show them the way out of the woods. The guru answers: "That I cannot do. But I can point out the ways that lead further into the thicket, and after that let us try to find the way together" (Kopp, 2013, p. 16). What an apt description of the supervisory process or journey that we existentially oriented supervisors often undertake with our supervisees. Intellectually, supervisees and their clients know that getting lost does not equate to failure. However, this truth must be embodied. For the best way for our supervisees to learn about the value of being lost is to have the experience of being accompanied while being lost together with their supervisor. Much easier said than done.

Such supervisee-centered principles are found throughout the Tao Te Ching, which addresses three topics: Natural law, a way of life that is in harmony with natural law, and leadership in the sense of how to govern or educate others in accordance with natural law. In regard to leadership, there is much resonance between Taoist principles and the aforementioned attitudes when it comes to supervision from an existential–humanistic perspective. For example:

Tao Te Ching, Verse 17

True leaders
are hardly known to their followers.
Next after them are the leaders
the people know and admire;
after them, those they fear;
after them, those they despise.

To give no trust
is to get no trust.

When the work's done right,
with no fuss or boasting,
ordinary people say,
Oh, we did it. (Lao Tzu, 2009, p. 27)

Tao Te Ching, Verse 65 (excerpts)

The ancient ones were simple-hearted
 And blended with the common people
They did not shine forth
They did not rule with cleverness
 So the nation was blessed

Now the rulers are filled with clever ideas
 and the lives of people are filled with hardship
 So the nation is cursed. (Lao Tzu, 2003, p. 78)

Tao Te Ching, Verse 66

The Rivers and the Seas (because they seek a lowly place) are Lords of a hundred valleys
Let your love flow, seek a lowly place, you will be Lord of a hundred valleys.
That is why if the self-controlled man desires to exalt the people, in his speech he must take a lowly place; if he desires to put the people first he must put himself after them.
Thus, though he dwells above them, the people are not burdened by him

> Though he is placed before them, the people are not obstructed by him,
> Therefore men serve him gladly, they do not tire in serving him.
> Because he does not strive, no one in the world can strive against him. (Lao Tzu, 2012, Chapter 6, para. 66)

Tao Te Ching, Verse 78 (excerpts)

> Of the soft and weak things in the world
> None is weaker than water.
> But in overcoming that which is firm and strong
> Nothing can equal it.
> It is easy to know the inner meaning of this: "That which is weak conquers the strong, that which is soft conquers the hard."
> All men know this, No one is able to practice it. (Lao Tzu, 2012, Chapter 6, para. 78)

Old men see visions and young men dream dreams (Acts 2:17). Good supervisors are those with a vision of the supervisee's potential while helping to actualize her dreams. True to the spirit of humanistic psychology, a good supervisor is one who will endeavor to liberate or inspire the supervisee not to follow in the supervisor's footsteps but to fulfill his or her potential and become who he or she is meant to be. Indeed the goal of supervision is to return the supervisee to herself. In the words of Nietzsche, to "become yourself" or to "consummate your life" (as cited in Yalom, 1992). Becoming oneself is rather straightforward and inane if you think about it. How can we be anyone else, but ourselves? Yet, this seemingly simple task, that of becoming oneself, is a life-long pursuit. Similarly in supervision and therapy, authenticity, congruence, integrity, or becoming oneself is exactly the end-point of training. It begins with the examination of oneself, often a painful process of deconstruction. Then it's about making oneself over to that helpful person, the expert technician—a process of reconstruction. Many will misunderstand this to be the end goal. How enjoyable to be recognized as the expert authority figure. However, the end point is not to become or model ourselves after some external admired authority figure; instead it is to come full circle and become oneself—to reclaim that beginner's mind, the passion, the simple wisdom of the original innocent self. It involves emptying and a willingness to enter into the unknown. This is the most difficult undertaking in the entire developmental process, the challenge of returning to oneself. And heaven knows that self at the beginning is significantly different from the self at the end (Dias, 2017). This recalls the popular Zen saying:

> Before I had studied Zen for thirty years, I saw mountains as mountains, and rivers as rivers. When I arrived at a more intimate knowledge, I came to the point where I saw that mountains are not mountains, and rivers are not rivers. But now that I have got its very substance I am at rest. For it's just that I see mountains once again as mountains, and rivers once again as rivers." (Qingyuan Weixin, 1949)

Many have asked me when I became an existential psychotherapist? The simple answer is after I begin reading Irvin Yalom's teaching novels after graduate school. However, in the process of *selfing* (Craig, 2000), I've come to discover that I was an existentialist all along. I remember enjoying solitude in the fringes of community during my youth. I preferred watching the stars and "vegging" with my friends in high school rather than partying it up. I recall sitting in the car in high school comforting a friend after his break up with his girlfriend. I was being with and encountering the I–Thou well before reading about such concepts in my graduate studies. Such was the I, the self at the beginning. Furthermore, regarding the spiritual or transpersonal, I argue that I was destined to be an existential psychologist before I was born. Existential psychology is my vocation and calling. But this vocation required systematic training and thus began the deconstruction of the mountains and rivers. I learned the technical skills of active listening and empathy. I tried to become a technical expert, nearly at the cost of my soul. People became cases and phenomena became syndromes. Fortunately, I returned to myself, striving to actualize the name preceding the titles rather than the titles themselves. Even though the destination was the same, the self I returned to full circle is vastly different from the self at the beginning. I'm still sitting beside and being with, but the quality of that companionship is different. And I'm still "selfing" for "selfing" is a verb and not a noun. It is an endless process of construction and deconstruction, filling and emptying. The circle is like a wheel, turning over and over, bringing me closer to an aspirational self that I will never achieve. The middle stage of skills building is important but must not be mistaken for the end goal. It is sad if supervision and an advanced degree were merely about deconstruction and reconstruction along with the mastery of skill without coming around full circle and returning to the supervisee's authentic self. For the essence of being far and away trumps the busyness of doing. So it is the supervisee's self, her soul, her being that we must develop if she is to become a helpful healer.

In the supervisory process, we are like midwives. Yalom (2002) suggested that therapists are midwives to their client's unborn self. Similarly, a good supervisor must help her supervisees hear their own voices and realize their own potential. For neophyte therapists, supervisors must understand their responsibility because they hold the fragile ego of the young supervisees in their hands. Like a young infant's, that ego is fragile and requires much encouragement. I've come to develop a healthy respect for the resilience of many neophyte therapists. I've borne witness to that resilience on many occasions when supervisees unburdened to me their having to survive the inexperience or lack of awareness of a number of their previous supervisors. My journey was no different. It appears that there is a disproportionate number of neophyte supervisors supervising neophyte supervisees in practicum settings. This often results in scarring on the part of numerous supervisees in training. We hold the fragile ego of the developing neophyte therapist in our hands. and we must recognize our roles as midwives and provide sufficient encouragement and nurturance of the birthing of the therapists who are newly becoming.

Yalom is not the only one to employ the metaphor of the midwife. Socrates also employed this metaphor as a way of communicating just what it is that he does when he teaches younger men. Socrates revealed that he was the son of a "brave and burly" midwife named Phaenarete and that he himself was a practitioner of midwifery. Socrates points out that Artemis, the goddess of childbirth, is not herself a mother. It makes her sympathetic to women who are barren but she will not allow them to be midwives for "human nature cannot know the mystery of art without experience." Therefore, Artemis makes the wise compromise of assigning the office of midwife to women who are past the age of bearing children of their own. The same metaphor applies to Socrates, who was also too old to create and produce ideas of his own. Instead, he was midwife to the ideas of others, tending to men rather than women; and it is their souls that are in labor rather than their bodies. Some young men who seek him are barren of ideas. Thus, Socrates must coax them into relationships that will stimulate them to become creative. He must be a cunning matchmaker with the knowledge of unions that will likely to be fruitful.

> And should a young man be pregnant with an idea when he comes to be taught by Socrates, or should he become so through his teacher's matchmaking, then Socrates, the midwife, knows how to induce labor, how to "arouse the pangs and to soothe them." The midwife goes on to help in the delivery, but it must be remembered that the child is not his. So it is that those who converse with Socrates profit from being with him. Still he insists that they never really learn anything from him. He merely helps them to discover the ideas already growing within them. Of course, he does reserve the right to inspect the fetus and to watch for signs of deformity. Then if he thinks fit, as the midwife, he "can smother the embryo in the womb." He asks that the young men do not quarrel with him over such judgments of their conceptions, but he points out, "there are some who were ready to bite me when I deprive them of a darling folly." (Kopp, 1972, pp. 74–75)

Watching out for signs of deformity and smothering the embryo in the womb. Such horrid imagery, but an apt description of the occasional agonizing and tormenting decisions courageous supervisors make when they decide to fail a supervisee. Yes, bite marks are part of the wounds of a midwife/supervisor!

It is the rare instance when midwives must smother an embryo in the womb. Most of the time, midwives create a supervisory space that is characterized by Khora, an ancient Greek term used by Plato to designate a receptacle. Plato's characterized Khora as neither being or non-being, but an interval between. It receives all, gives space and has maternal overtones (womb). In this space characterized by Khora, we would give primacy to questions instead of privileging answers. The supervision would be relative and flexible where unknowing and uncertainty are experienced as the norm rather than flaws. The supervisor would model all of this by himself or herself surrendering to the process and releasing control. Instead of fixing the supervisee's shortcomings, the supervisor and supervisee would together explore the supervisee's struggles, allowing the process to unfold and seeking understanding rather than prescribing correction. Khora would make room for mistakes, imperfections, anxiety, pain, and transformation.

Most important, this form of Khora-based supervision and therapy must be embodied for the supervisee. Just as it is with lived meaning, the supervision must be alive and the embodied concepts lived out. Mere instruction is simply not enough (Todd Dubose, Personal Communication, March 27, 2018).

Finally, descriptions of Taoist principles applied to supervision are wonderfully illustrated in the following Taoist tale about effective leadership found in Phil Jackson's (2013) book *Eleven Rings.* The tale illustrates the principle that a leader/supervisor is like a shepherd. He stays behind the flock, letting the most nimble go out ahead, whereupon the others follow, not realizing that all along they are being directed from behind. Emperor Liu Bang was an exceptional leader who consolidated China into a unified empire in the third century BC. He held a banquet to celebrate his victory and invited many dignitaries, one of which was Chen Cen who provided Liu Bang with much guidance during the unification campaign. Chen Cen's disciples accompanied him to the banquet but were perplexed by the seating arrangements at the head table. The disciples recognized a number of illustrious figures, including military commanders and diplomats, but were puzzled by Liu Bang's position as the emperor for he was not of noble birth and did not possess any obvious knowledge or skills. Recognizing their bewilderment, Chen Cen asked his disciples to think about what gives strength to a wheel. One disciple replied the sturdiness of the spokes. But Chen Cen reminded them that two wheels made of identical spokes can differ in strength. He goes on to say:

> See beyond what is seen. Never forget that a wheel is made not only of spokes but also of the space between the spokes. Sturdy spokes poorly placed make a weak wheel. Whether the full potential is realized depends on the harmony between. The essence of wheel-making lies in the craftsman's ability to conceive and create the space that holds and balances the spokes within the wheel. Think now, who is the craftsman here?
>
> -------------
>
> Chen Cen then asked them to think of sunlight. "The sun nurtures and vitalizes trees and flowers," he said. "It does so by giving away its light. But in the end, in which direction do they grow? So it is with a master craftsman in life Liu Bang. After placing individuals in positions that fully realize their potential, he secures harmony among them by giving them full credit for

> their distinctive achievements. And in the end, as the tree and flowers grow toward the giver, the sun, individuals grow towards Liu Bang with devotion (Jackson & Delehanty, 2013, p. 161).

Parallel Process and Embodiment

How are we to become midwives to our supervisees' process of selfing? It is the same process of how we teach or model for our supervisees how to nurture the nascent selves of their clients. Our task is not so much to teach as to guide. Teaching is part of the job description, but the supervisees will develop more quickly and successfully if we guide them along rather than simply telling them what to do. Just as it is with our clients, this requires more listening than instructing for too much instruction will overwhelm and impede the growth of our supervisees. Just as for our clients, it is very important to provide space and time for the supervisee to talk, at the expense of instruction (when they are not ready to receive), so that their professional selves may be formed. It is important that we allow our supervisees to talk as opposed to listening to ourselves talk. It is the ego of our supervisees and not our own egos that are to be developed. Kahlil Gibran (2015) understood the same when he wrote the following poem *On Teaching*:

> No man can reveal to you aught
> but that which already lies half asleep in the dawning of our knowledge.
> The teacher who walks in the shadow of the temple, among his followers,
> gives not of his wisdom but rather of his faith and his lovingness.
>
> If he is indeed wise he does not bid you to enter the house of wisdom,
> but rather leads you to the threshold of your own mind.
> The astronomer may speak to you of his understanding of space,
> but he cannot give you his understanding.
> The musician may sing to you of the rhythm which is in all space,

> but he cannot give you the ear which arrests the rhythm nor
> the voice that echoes it.
>
> And he who is versed in the sciences of numbers can tell of the
> regions of weight and measure,
> but he cannot conduct you thither.
>
> For the vision of one man lends not its wings to another man.
>
> And even as each of you stands alone in God's knowledge,
> so must each of you be alone in his knowledge of God and in
> his understanding of the earth. (pp. 32–33)

In addition to listening, the transmission of knowledge must involve embodiment, embodying the essential, intangible elements of the art of psychotherapy as opposed to direct instruction. How do we "teach" our supervisees about authenticity and empathy? Conceptually, these concepts can be conveyed didactically. But that only goes so far. When "a way that can be walked is not the Way and a name that can be named is not The Name" (Lao Tzu, 2003, p.5), we are left with experience. It is critical that we embody the Way, and trust that each supervisee will individually take away what they need. We cannot give our experience to our supervisees. In fact, the harder we try to pass on empathy or authenticity, the more we're likely to fail in our endeavor. Like the lessons taught by my ballroom dance instructor advised, lead your partner through giving the energy and force to yourself and be responsible for your own weight transfer. Consequently, your partner will receive the necessary energy, force, direction, and movement to allow her to initiate her own movement. The more you try to lead through giving her your weight, the more uncomfortable she will be. This truth must be embodied. It must be experienced, so my instructor had me dance the part of the female partner and had me feel in my body the two different approaches to leading. My understanding deepened considerably after physically experiencing the difference. Similarly, this was embodied for me in an instant when a friend offered her hand to help me climb a steep dirt incline while hiking. She meant well when she stretched out her hand and began to pull me up in an effort to assist. However, what I experienced was terror. I was already unbalanced and her strong pull nearly toppled me. Instead, what I needed was her grounded stillness. I needed her to remain still, concentrating her energy on herself, anchoring herself to the earth and thus allowing me to pull myself up when I was ready. Simple in concept but difficult to practice when we'll full of desire to help.

In regard to anchoring, stillness and the transmission of special skills to another, Zhuangzi (1998) wrote the following parable. Paradoxically, we may be able to effect the best movement in our supervisees if we are focused and anchored in the basics:

> When Confucius was traveling in Ch'u, he passed through a woods and saw there a hunchback catching cicadas at the end of a long, sticky pole as easily as if he were gathering them up with his hands.
>
> "That's quite a skill you have!" said Confucius. "Is there a special way to do it?"
>
> "I have a way. For five or six months, I practice balancing two pellets at the end of my pole. When I can keep them from falling down, then I'll only lose a small fraction of the cicadas. When I can balance three balls and keep them from falling down, then I'll only lose one cicada in ten. When I can balance five balls and keep them from falling down, then I can gather up the cicadas as easily as if I were using my hands. I position my body as though it were an erect stump with twisted roots. I hold my arms as though they were the branches of a withered tree. The greatness of heaven and earth and the numerousness of the myriad things notwithstanding, I am aware of only the cicada's wings. I neither turn around nor to the side and wouldn't exchange the wings of a cicada for all the myriad things. How can I not succeed?"
>
> Confucius turned to his disciples, "In exercising your will, do not let it be diverted; concentrate your spirit. This is the lesson of the hunchback gentleman." (pp. 176–177)[2]

So how do we be a good leader when dancing? How do we help to help lift someone up in their times of need? How do we teach authenticity and empathy? The principle is the same. Be an anchor and focus the energy and intention on oneself. Embody the truth of authenticity and empathy, trust the process and our supervisees to pick up what they need in their own way at their own pace. A friend once

---

[2] Permission to republish granted by the University of Hawaii Press. Zhuangzi, (1998). *Wandering on The Way: Early Taoist Tales and Parables of Chuang Tzu.* (V. Mair, Trans.). Honolulu, HI: University of Hawaii Press.

told me, "Once you know who you are, then the rest of the world will find out." If we are clear about who we *are* as supervisors, then our supervisees can learn about how to become themselves through our embodiment of this basic truth.

Tao Te Ching, Verse 33

> He who knows men is wise,
> He who knows himself can see clearly.
> He who conquers men has strength,
> He who conquers himself has power
> He who knows that he has enough is rich,
> He who acts with energy has a strong will.
> He who fails not to find the Self shall endure,
> He who dies, but does not perish, shall endure for ever. (Lao Tzu, 2012, Chapter 6, para. 33)

The gains in therapy and supervision are progressive and incremental. Each session can simply be only a tiny small part of the whole. Lessons need to be repeated over and over again. Jacob Riis (n.d.) a 19th century social reformer shared:

> When nothing seems to help, I go look at a stonecutter hammering away at his rock perhaps a hundred times without as much as a crack showing in it. Yet at the hundred-and-first blow it will split in two, and I know it was not that blow that did it, but all that had gone before.

The same principle applies in boxing where everyone is looking for that knockout blow. But the boxer, as opposed to the puncher, knows that the knockout punch is effective because of the numerous jabs that have been delivered over the course of the bout. The jab is not sexy but is beautiful to the boxing technician. Similarly, T. S. Elliot, as cited in Rollo May (1969, p. 202), wrote:

> Between the conception
> And the creation
> Between the emotion
> And the response
> Falls the Shadow
> Life is very long

Yet, when embodied, the whole becomes mysteriously greater than the sum of its parts. The lessons from this subsection are nicely summarized in another memorable story by Dr. Remen (2000) about a gift from her grandfather. The gift was a clear plastic glass that contained a seed. When she wanted to know what kind of seed it was, her grandfather merely said, "Make sure it's watered and has plenty of sun, and you'll find out." Rachel dutifully did as her grandfather requested, and eventually she saw a little sprout. She called him on the telephone and again asked what it was. Same answer. Every time she called, she asked the same question, and each time her grandfather's answer was the same. Our supervisees are a lot like that seed. We have an idea but cannot know for sure how they will turn out. And we certainly cannot make them into therapists that we want (thank God!), but we can love and nurture them nonetheless.

> How did the rose ever open its heart
> And give to this world all of its beauty?
> It felt the encouragement of light against its being.
> Otherwise we all remain too frightened. (Hafiz, 2010)

Bearing Witness

In addition, we are to "bear witness" to our supervisees' development just as they bear witness to their client's growth. We act as our supervisee's historians, holding on to hope and perspective, to a vision of themselves greater than they can imagine, just as they do the same for their clients. We chart their growth as they chart their clients' growth. We remember the details of the stories/cases they tell us. We understand that part of their clients' stories is their story, just as part of their story is our story. They are touched when we remember. In the details of what we remember, our clients and supervisees come into existence. They are seen, they are valued, they exist! When it comes to termination, while we're teaching our supervisees to review and consolidate their clients' growth, keep in mind that they are reviewing and consolidating their own development as well in the process. Their professional selves are growing along with their clients' selves. Indeed this is one of the most enjoyable aspects of my role as a supervisor, mentor, and leader.

It is immensely satisfying for me to bear witness to my student's growth and development. I am a proud parent. After graduation, when looking back, I'll reminisce with my ex-supervisees, now colleagues, the path they've traversed to become the professionals that they now are. I am their historian. Their growth continues in my eyes though our relationship has changed. Nevertheless, my admiration remains important. We'll recall their personal essays and their entrance interviews. We'll relive the highlights and challenges of their clinical training. My supervisees will often remind me of things that I said that have long escaped my memory. Fortuitous seeds unknowingly planted germinating all along under my supervisory nurturance and guidance. They invite me out for coffee and share with me the challenges of their new careers. They reward me with the ripples of my toils for now they have become supervisors in their own right. The cycle of life continues. Zhuangzi (2013) wrote that "though the grease burns out of the torch, the fire passes on, and no one knows where it ends" (Chapter 3, para. 15). Our supervision sessions have long passed, but the relationship continues. It remains important that I continue to bear witness to the developments in their lives. And as I think about it, writing this chapter is me bearing witness to my own development as a supervisor. The fire, the torch continues to burn. This is the beauty of what we do.

Stand Up, Now We Hug!

The power of the simple act of bearing witness can be illustrated in the following story that I was fortunate to be a part of. It is my honor to bear witness and record the heroic rebellion that a number of human rights lawyers and their assistants in Hong Kong are engaged in against evil and indifference—a heroic and even prideful rebellion advocated by the French existential philosopher Camus, who believed that human beings can attain full stature only by living with dignity in the face of absurdity. The tension between human aspiration (some would understand as folly) and the world's indifference is what Camus referred to as the "absurd" human condition. Nonetheless, the world's cruelty and indifference can be transcended by rebellion, a prideful rebellion against one's stark conditions.

One of the things that we existential psychologists take seriously is the existence of evil in the world. It is painful for me to reflect on how much evil and pain are perpetrated in the world for various reasons. The pain is such that I prefer not to think about it most of the time. When I do take time to reflect, I am baffled, angry, and exasperated with how much trauma and suffering is inflicted by a few upon so many, while it takes legions of heroic individuals to help just a few of these victims. What about justice? Where is the meaning in all this suffering?

Is there no meaning at all? It makes little sense to me. The philosophical and theological explanations regarding free will or God's will provide me with limited comfort. What make more sense to me are the words (The Copernicus Turn) of Victor Frankl (1985), who taught us in his book *Man's Search for Meaning*:

> As each situation in life represents a challenge to man and presents a problem for him to solve, the question of the meaning of life may actually be reversed. Ultimately, man should not ask what the meaning of his life is, but rather he must recognize that it is *he* who is asked. It does not really matter what we expect from life, but rather what life expects from us. In a word, each man is questioned by life; and he can only answer to life by answering *for* his own life; to life, he can only respond by being responsible. (p. 131)

What fosters my denial and avoidance is the sense of helplessness that I feel whenever I ponder the scope of the suffering that takes place. I loathe this feeling of helplessness. Yet, it is this same helplessness that lawyers at the Hong Kong Refugee Advice Center (HKRAC, http://www.hkrac.org/) face regularly. The unsung heroines at the HKRAC persist despite struggling with their own sense of helplessness every day. They consistently take on refugee cases applying for asylum even though at the outset they know that the cases have virtually no chance for success—a Sisyphus-like task. This also makes little financial sense. They invest a significant amount of time in these cases even though they know it will fail. Why? Why not? Because these compassionate and compassion-fatigued lawyers know that what they do is significant *just because*. They know that the meaning of what they do is not directly tied into whether their applications are successful. But try they must. It is a matter of rebellion in the face of absurdity! If they were solely dependent upon success, they'd all have quit in despair a long time ago. Even with successful applications, the journey has only begun. In the words of one attorney, "You can't control the outcome but you can give your client a good day."

In addition to protecting the refugees' legal rights and providing high-quality legal advice, the staff members help to preserve their clients' dignity. They do this by bearing witness and giving meaning to their clients' suffering. The briefs that they write are significant beyond the fact that they document the traumatic events that took place. Think of the vicarious trauma that the staff (lawyers, assistants, and translators) endure from hearing repeated details of systemic torture and abuse. The briefs are significant because they are a record of the narrative of the suffering that has been endured. They are significant because otherwise the suffering will be unheard, undocumented, invisible, and therefore non-existent. They battle against the pain of insignificance. The applications may ultimately be unsuccessful, but their clients are nevertheless tremendously grateful. Grateful that despite the evil that has been perpetrated upon them, there are others in the world who care enough to listen and bear witness to their suffering. The attorneys not only document; they also create worth. The documents are part of the legal system that may ultimately fail them, yet, psychologically, bearing witness to their pain creates worth, significance, and bonds of human connection in a desolate land of brokenness. Here I am reminded of Zhuangzi's tale of The Useless tree discussed in detail in Chapter One of my book *Existential Psychology and the Way of the Tao: Meditations on the Writings of Zhuangzi* (Yang, 2017).

> Master Hui said to Master Chuang, "I have a big tree people call Stinky Quassia. Its great trunk is so gnarled and knotted that it cannot be measured with an inked line. Its small branches are so twisted and turned that neither compass nor L-Square can be applied to them. It stands next to the road, but carpenters pay no attention to it. Now sir, your words are just like my tree —big, useless, and heeded by no one."
>
> "Sir," said Master Chuang, "are you the only one who hasn't observed a wild cat or a weasel? Crouching down, it lies in wait for its prey. It leaps about east and west, avoiding neither high nor low, until it gets caught in a snare or dies in a net. Then there is the yak, big as the cloud suspended in the sky. It's big, all right, but it can't catch mice. Now you, sir, have a big tree and are bothered by its uselessness. Why don't you plant it in the Never-never Land with its wide open spaces? There you can roam in non-action by its side and sleep carefreely beneath it. Your Stinky Quassia's life will not be cut short by axes, nor will anything else harm it. Being useless, how could it ever come to grief? (Zhuangzi, 1998, pp. 8–9)

Zhuangzi employed the metaphor of a big stinktree with its grotesque gnarls and knots to illustrate the fundamental value of existential worth. Gnarl and knots are part of existence, and it is precisely these unsightly characteristics that have become the secret to the tree's longevity. And last but not least, the beauty and utility of the "useless" stinktree lie in its ability to survive in the wasteland, providing shelter for those in their times of need.

Carl Rogers (1980) taught us that empathy dissolves alienation. Rogers learned this from Carl Jung, who was purported to say that "schizophrenics cease to be schizophrenic when they meet other persons by whom they feel understood" (p. 152). Through the staff's patient listening, the translator's faithful translation, and the attorney's sifting through the stories of trauma, the briefs written are Books of Life. When successfully recognized by the legal system, they provide a chance for new life. Regardless of the results of the application for asylum, the briefs help to recreate meaningful existence for people whose lives have been ravaged by evil. And the amazing thing is, these highly qualified lawyers commit to this beautiful work for pitiful wages while living in Hong Kong, one of the most expensive cities in the world. How can I not bear witness and conduct my own recording of their heroic rebellion!

Despite the pitifully low wages, there are some fringe benefits. There is beauty in the midst of suffering. The staff shared one of these benefits with me recently when they fondly recalled the jubilations of one of their few successful applicants. The applicant ran into the office and exclaimed, "Stand Up, Now We Hug!" Imagine this being said with a heavy African accent. After years of struggle, what else can we say but "Stand Up, Now We Hug!"

Chapter 3

Bruce's Story: An Encounter Through Song

I've devoted the past twelve years of my life to the training and development of psychotherapists from an existential–humanistic perspective. To this end, I strongly believe in prioritizing the development of the person of the psychotherapist over the teaching of clinical skills. For if you believe in the psychotherapeutic principle of life impacting life, the most important "tool" in therapy being the person of the therapist, then naturally the development of one's self is critical. One of my supervisors is fond of reminding me that when it comes to qualifications, what matters most is not the titles or credentials but the person that precedes the titles. This is similar in principle to one of Carl Roger's (1980) most important teachings: What matters most in therapy is not what we must do, but how we must be. So it is our being, not our expert knowledge, not our training, not our techniques, that is the essential ingredient when it comes to psychological healing. This is the fundamental basis of existential–humanistic psychotherapy.

The concept that what is most important in therapy is not what we do but how we must be is illustrated in the following two stories. The first is a famous Chinese story of the three brothers who were all physicians. The youngest brother was asked which one amongst them was the best physician? He replied that his oldest brother was the best, followed by the middle brother, followed by himself. The one who made the inquiry was perplexed and asked the younger brother to explain. The younger brother enlightened the inquirer by pointing out that the eldest brother practiced prevention and addressed the roots of the problem. He worked in a subtle manner with people before the onset of disease. Therefore, his skills were difficult to recognize and thus did not become famous. The middle brother was successful because he was able to work with his patients during the onset of the disease when the pain was minor and the symptoms were not very obvious. Therefore, the people of the village thought that the middle brother was most suitable for treating "minor" ailments. I, on the other hand, treated the most serious diseases. Patients' families generally sought me out when they were desperate with the patient in extreme distress. People see me applying obvious and tangible interventions such as checking the meridians, prescribing medications, resecting lesions, and performing surgery. The patients generally experienced immediate relief and this is why I became famous.

Then there is the story of The Holy Shadow as told by Osho (Rajneesh, 1981).

> There once lived a saint so good that the angels came from heaven to see how a man could be so godly. This saint went about his daily life diffusing virtue as the stars diffuse light and the flowers scent, without being aware of it. His day could be summed up by two words — he gave, he forgave — yet these words never passed his lips. They were expressed in his ready smile, his kindness, forbearance, and charity
>
> The angels said to God, "Lord, grant him the gift of miracles."
>
> God replied, "Ask what it is that he wishes."
>
> They said to the saint, "Would you like the touch of your hands to heal the sick?"
>
> "No," answered the saint. "I would rather God do that."
>
> "Would you like to convert guilty souls and bring back wandering hearts to the right path?"
>
> "No, that is the angels' mission. It is not for me to convert."
>
> "Would you like to become a model of patience, attracting men by the luster of your virtues, and thus glorifying God?"
>
> "No," replied the saint. "If men should be attracted to me, they would become estranged from God." "What is it that you desire, then?" asked the angels.
>
> "What can I wish for?" asked the saint smiling. "That God gives me his grace; with that would I not have everything?" The angels said, "You must ask for a miracle, or one will be forced upon you."
>
> "Very well," said the saint. "That I may do a great deal of good without ever knowing it."
>
> The angels were perplexed. They took counsel and resolved upon the following plan: every time the saint's shadow fell behind him or to either side, so that he could not

> see it, it would have the power to cure disease, soothe pain, and comfort sorrow. (p. 137)

Letting Go

One of the first things that I try to accomplish right from the start with all of my supervisees is to encourage them to let go. This is incredibly difficult to accomplish and counterintuitive, not only for beginning trainees but for myself as well. Letting go is a continuous, painful lesson that all of us have encountered. Letting go has to do with the existential givens of transience and impermanence, the basic tenets of Buddhism. I mouth this to myself whenever I encounter the change that is ubiquitous and unavoidable in developing economies of China and parts of Southeast Asia. Many of the coastal big cities in China are founded on the backs of migrant workers. And migration involves transition. Living here in China, I have come to expect this migratory change. During a previous trip to Shenzhen, the large Chinese city bordering Hong Kong, I went out expecting my usual haircut followed by lunch at my familiar noodle shop. I made a special trip on the subway to visit both of these establishments only to find them replaced with a lottery ticket shop and a fast-food chain store. Transience and impermanence, transience and impermanence, I repeated to myself. This mantra helped to soothe my disappointment until I realized that I, too, was part of that migration for I, too, have moved on from Hong Kong and Shenzhen. So what right did I have to expect the barbershop and noodle shop to remain in place for me? Yet, that was exactly what I wanted. Intellectually I understood transience and impermanence, but emotionally I wanted familiarity and predictability. What I found instead were lottery tickets and fast food.

This sense of impermanence followed me as I continued my visit to Malaysia. I found out from Evone, a good Malaysian friend and fellow existentialist that Coffee Famille, a coffee shop close to my heart that I presented in the introductory chapter, was also due to close. I protested to Evone, "No more closures! Enough transience for one trip!" Where is my happy ending? I need familiarity and predictability. I asked Evone, who wrote her master's thesis at Coffee Famille, what happened? She encouraged me to visit Ving and ask for myself. So that is exactly what I did.

Without thinking too much, I prepared for disappointment and a heavy dose of reality. After all, it is not easy to survive standing out from the crowd. Dreams eventually come to an end, don't they? What I found instead was additional inspiration and, thankfully, the continuation of a story instead of the end. Ving offered Evone and me a warm greeting and immediately offered us two cups of coffee made expertly without delay. Evone had her usual Sweet Dream and Ving suggested that I try Homey Latte. After we sat down with our coffees, Ving revealed that she was closing her café because she wanted to become a more dedicated barista! Huh? And here I thought this was the end of my barista heroine. She said that in order to become a better barista, she needed to learn to become a roaster and source her own beans. Ving told us that it was no longer enough to purchase beans from others and roast her small quantities for her own shop. To become a good roaster, she needed to go to the plantations, talk to the farmers, and understand the beans at its source. She could not see herself operating a café and sourcing her own beans at the same time. Ving wanted to dedicate herself to roasting. She understood that in order to do this, she needed to let go of the café and make a commitment to roasting. Her dedication and clarity of purpose had not only remained unchanged, but it also had deepened, evidence of further growth along her journey.

I tested Ving's resolve. I asked her why she had to sell her café. After all, what about all the work she invested in building up her clientele? Clientele who grew along with her to appreciate not only a good cup of coffee but the inner focus cultivated in the process of brewing. Ving inspired a few of her customers to buy their own equipment and roast their own coffee at home. Ving shared that this was indeed her biggest loss, for there were a few dear customers who grew along with Ving and developed the knowledge and palates to appreciate the subtle advancement that was evidence of Ving's improvement as a barista. Ving shared how she was able to taste the subtle difference in her improvement over the past seven years, which told her paradoxically that she had much more room to grow. "I thought I knew coffee then. Now I know how much I need to grow." And to achieve such growth, she needed to let the dream of her café and her regular customers go so that she could continue along that journey of growth.

Ving's dedication and pursuit of becoming a better barista are admirable and a lesson for us all who want to become a better therapist. The title of one of Carl Rogers (1961) books, *On Becoming A Person*, comes to mind, for along the journey of becoming a better therapist one soon realizes that it requires becoming a better person. Going back to the source. A life-long journey. To become one with the beans, it is not enough that we roast our own beans. To become one with our being, we need to go back to the source. We all start by learning techniques with perhaps a rudimentary understanding of theory. However, the efficacy of the technique lies in how one understands and embodies the essential basis behind the technique. And if we go further, we will realize that it is not about techniques, for there are myriad ways to embody the essential elements that lead to healing. Eventually, the techniques disappear or become internalized, as the Taoists would say, such that one can no longer tell the fiddle apart from the fiddler or the sword apart from the swordsman. They've become one, both nothing and everything. The Kung Fu master no longer focuses on the weaponry for they are mere tools. To strike with force requires a firm foundation involving our feet, knees, hips, shoulders, not just our arm and fists. Existential psychology is not a psychological orientation but a way of life, something that Ving embodies in her dedication to becoming a barista.

Back in Malaysia. Ving reminded me that letting go does not equal failure. It is an unavoidable part of growth. She reminded me again of the well-known Buddhist Parable of the Raft where we must let go of our hard-earned investments in the past in order to move on toward the possibilities of the future.

> A man traveling along a path came to a great expanse of water. As he stood on the shore, he realized there were dangers and discomforts all about. But the other shore appeared safe and inviting.
>
> The man looked for a boat or a bridge and found neither. But with great effort he gathered grass, twigs and branches and tied them all together to make a simple raft. Relying on the raft to keep himself afloat, the man paddled with his hands and feet and reached the safety of the other shore. He could continue his journey on dry land.
>
> Now, what would he do with his makeshift raft? Would he drag it along with him or leave it behind? He would leave it, the Buddha said. Then the Buddha explained that the dharma is like a raft. It is useful for crossing over but not for holding onto, he said. (O'Brien, 2016)

Finally, here is an additional story by Sheldon Kopp (2013) regarding the necessity of letting go in order to move forward. Freedom and enlightenment are often present but unreachable by us because of our very efforts to try to attain them. There was a man who imagined himself imprisoned in a cell. He'd stand on his tiptoes, arms stretched upward, grasping the bars of a small window and yearning for the light outside his cell. By holding on tight, straining towards the window, he'd barely see a few rays of sunlight through the uppermost bars. Sunlight was the hope he'd dare not lose. Sadly, because he was committed in his effort not to lose the sliver of light, it never occurred to him to let go and explore the darkness of the rest of his cell. In letting go, he'd discover the open door on the other end of his cell. He'd always been free to walk into the sunshine if he'd only be willing to let go.

Dialogues in the Dark

The story of letting go involving the prisoner in the darkened cell reminded me of an interactive exhibit a friend and I visited in New York titled *Dialogues in The Dark* (http://www.dialogue-in-the-dark.com). It was an "illuminating" experience for us to enter into the world of the blind. Though the experience was fun for me, I can only imagine what it would be like to have lost my sight permanently. Yet, as I was trying not to pity the blind, our blind guide reminded us that what the disabled need is our offer of help and not our pity. Each disabled person can then make their own decisions as to whether to accept our help or not. He demonstrated this physically by teaching us how to offer ourselves as a guide for the blind. Prior to this lesson, I was unaware and gave this process little thought. Without the lesson, I might have in haste grabbed the blind person's hand and then proceeded to lead the way. Instead, our guide taught us that all we have to do is to offer our arm and wait for the blind person to reach out for that offer of help. Or not. They can feel our presence and gauge the space between us. There is a process of give and take. Our job is to offer, to trust the process, and allow the blind person to reach out across space to find our arm and the comfortable distance that he or she needs. Surely, we can all identify the basic humanistic principles at play here when it comes to the offering of guidance, physically or psychologically.

The interactive exhibit began with a few existentially oriented quotes that were pleasantly surprising for me. The first by the existential Hebrew theologian Martin Buber put everything in context: "Encounter is the only possible way of learning." The quote was especially meaningful to me for the authentic therapist–client encounter is the essence of existential–humanistic psychotherapy. Furthermore, the quote took on concrete, kinesthetic, and tactile meaning for me when I had to discover, encounter, and trust everything I came across in the dark through my other sense organs beside my eyes.

Our guide, well at home in the dark (a nice metaphor for existential therapists), kept on reminding us to let go of our desire to "see" with our eyes. He taught us over and over again that the sooner we can let go of our desire to return to the familiarity of seeing with our eyes, the more we will discover the amazing acuity present in our other senses. It quickly became an exercise in mindful walking as I felt anew the texture and sensation of gravel, grass, and carpet. I also amazed myself with my keen sense of hearing. How quickly I was able to identify sounds that were previously lingering in the background. It reminded me of the different realms of awareness that are always available to us. It's always been a matter of attunement, of what we choose to pay attention to. The foreground became background, and phenomenon that was always present came to the fore. It was an awakening of sorts. Finally, a whole new world of scents entered into my awareness. Having to rely on my nose helped me to appreciate the olfactory assortment that dogs enjoy during their walks (when I stop yanking on their chains). Knowing this admonishes me to learn from my furry friends about how to slow down and "smell the roses" for there is a parallel universe out there waiting to be discovered, if I can slow down and change channels!

The experience gave me a new insight into the following famous quote titled "A Generation" (一代) from the contemporary Chinese poet Gu Chen (2005): "The Dark Night blackens my eyes, I, nonetheless, use them to seek for light (黑夜给了我黑色的眼睛，我却用它寻找光明)" (p. IX). Even though Gu Chen referred to his blackened eyes to seek for light, perhaps the new eyes that he wrote about refers to the "third eye" or "third ear" that we seek to develop in our supervisees. Certainly, this experience embodied for me the necessity of letting go of our old pair of eyes and learning to trust our other senses. Similarly, Marcel Proust (1993) famously wrote that the real voyage of discovery consists not in seeking new landscapes but in having new eyes. On an even more basic level, my dialogues in the dark and Gu Chen's quote taught me that it is possible to find light amid darkness, but it requires letting go. For the Persian proverb teaches us that only when the night is dark enough do we then see the stars.

All of these experiences described above have obvious parallels to supervision and therapy. I will briefly share some of the lessons I learned here. First of all, my dialogue with the dark reminded me to "see beyond the obvious." It reinforced for me the lesson told by Antoine de Saint-Exupery (2000) in *The Little Prince*: "One sees clearly only with the heart. Anything essential is invisible to the eye" (p. 63). This is the same idea expressed by Stevie Wonder (blind musician) in a second quote displayed at the exhibit: "Just because a man lacks the use of his eyes does not mean he lacks vision." Second, it taught me that true seeing (and listening) requires letting go. Letting go of what we know so that we can enter into the realm of un-knowing, to discover things anew, a state of openness described by the British existential phenomenological therapist Ernesto Spinelli (1997). Finally, I learned that I need to slow down and take it slow, especially in the dark, if I am to enter into that parallel universe, that different realm of consciousness that is so vital if I am to dwell in the Ontological Way of Being. All critical skills to pass on to our supervisees.

In addition, I learned that being in darkness draws people together. This is better expressed in the third quote by Helen Keller that I encountered in the exhibit: "Walking with a friend in the dark is better than walking alone in the light." I entered the exhibit with a set of strangers who also came to visit the exhibit. Naturally, we kept our distance and were respectfully in our own spaces while in the light of the waiting area. However, once the lights were turned off, the distance evaporated. We were forced to communicate with one another actively in order to avoid bumping into one another while everyone negotiated the numerous "blind alleys" in the exhibit. And without the aid of our eyes, we had to "see" and feel with our hands and this naturally led to more physical encounters than we planned for. In the world of light, our physical encounters might be interpreted as groping. However, in the dark, they became probes of necessity. I lack sufficient experience of walking in the dark to fully appreciate Helen Keller's quote. My one-hour (it felt like ten minutes for I was fully engaged in the present) entry into the world of the blind gave me a "glimpse" of what she meant. Nevertheless, it helped me to appreciate the importance of friendships and guides amid the darkness, for I cannot imagine how I could possibly negotiate the world of darkness without the constant reassuring voice of our guide. His constant advice to seek his voice and pay attention to the vital directions given by him helped me to understand with greater depth the verse in Psalm 23 of the Bible about how the rod of the shepherd comforts the lost sheep.

The constant reassuring voice of our guide is an excellent model for how we are to guide our supervisees. This is explicated further in Tracy's Story: Steadiness in the Midst of Chaos, the next chapter in the book. In the midst of intense anxiety, often it is simply our voice as a reassuring presence, that our supervisees seek. When clients are lost, we teach our supervisees to be present and be willing to be lost with them. When our supervisees are lost, my experience and our blind guide taught me that we can often demonstrate presence by simply reassuring our supervisees that in the midst of darkness, though they may not see us, our support and presence will be with them as they enter the dark worlds of their clients. This has been proven true on numerous occasions when I served as that constant point of contact for supervisees who had to deal with the frightening anxiety of their client's suicidal crisis.

Finally, I could not help but think that during my one hour of dialoguing with the dark, it was indeed the blind leading the blind. Except, our blind guide was at home in the darkness, and the reassuring guidance he provided felt incredibly nurturing. This reminds me of the teaching of Victor Frankl (1985), who taught us that even though we are in the dark ourselves in regard to meaning—and to be sure, we cannot tell our clients or our supervisees what the meaning of their suffering is—what we can do is to carry on in the midst of darkness as that blind guide, offering confidence and reassurance that *there is* meaning in the process and that all we endure is part of our learning. It's another way of saying, trust in the process. The steadying voice of the guide told me not only which way to go, but through the calming attitude he espoused, I was assured that as long as I continued to walk forward step by step, I would eventually find a way out. And indeed if we have walked through the darkness before, we will most likely be a more confident guide to our supervisees, assuring them that the dialogues we have in the dark are meaningful and that things will be all right in the end.

Letting Go of Techniques

What is it that supervisees must let go of? As countless therapists and supervisors have taught, we must learn our techniques well but let go of them during the session. Ernesto Spinelli (2005) emphasizes that rather than any particular technique or method of therapy, existential psychotherapy provides therapists with a set of foundational principles or guidelines and meaning structures that underlie its practice. In fact, any over-emphasis on technique in general is likely to become an obstacle to understanding the client. "It is not the understanding that follows technique, but the technique that follows understanding" (Misiak & Sexton, 1973, p. 87). Yalom (2002) will always emphasize to his supervisees not to practice various techniques that were discussed during the supervisory session in the next session with their clients because the critical element of timing will likely be off. For those starting with few skills, if one has only a hammer then everything looks like a nail. The best rationale I heard for letting go of techniques came from a student during the First International Conference on Existential Psychology held in Nanjing China in 2009. In her quiet and yet strong voice, she taught the audience that if you let go of (a particular) technique, then all techniques become available to you. This was so beautifully Taoist. She must have been thinking about verse 38 of the Tao Te Ching, which suggests that, paradoxically, the highest virtue is non-action (Wu Wei, 无为), yet nothing is undone (德上德无为， 无以为). She went on to talk about Zhuangzi's (1998) concept of relative gradation (in chapter 17 of the book Zhuangzi titled *Autumn Floods*): A river may be relatively small compared to the sea; however, in the grand scheme of things, both are small relative to the entire cosmos. Therefore, she may be a blade grass compared to the other experts in the field; yet in the vast field of psychological knowledge, we are all students in our own right. The conference brought together leaders in the field of existential psychology from the East and the West. However, it was the wisdom of this small blade of grass that has stayed with me until now. Such is the way of the Tao: Though small and insignificant, indeed nothing under heaven can harness this pure and simple uncarved block (Tao Te Ching, verse 32 excerpts, 朴虽小天下， 莫能臣也).

Zhuangzi (2013) understood the limitation of techniques when he wrote the following parable:

> The fish trap exists because of the fish; once you've gotten the fish, you can forget the trap. The rabbit snare exists because of the rabbit; once you've gotten the rabbit, you can forget the snare. Words exist because of meaning; once you've gotten the meaning, you can forget the words. Where can I find a man who has forgotten words so I can have a word with him? (Chapter 26, para. 34)

Finally, as the Buddha taught in the Parable of the Raft above, do not forget to leave the raft behind after crossing the river lest it become an impediment to your continuing journey.

Letting Go of Goals

Along with the letting go of techniques, students also need to learn to let go of goals. But what is the purpose of therapy or how is one to conduct therapy without goals! Goals can get in the way. Once we set a goal for ourselves or the client, we begin to practice the technique with the purpose of attaining the goal. We are enticed to serve the goal instead of allowing the natural process to develop on its own. Many short-term solution-focused approaches to therapy will encourage the clients to develop a goal so as to gain focus and increase intentionality. This is typically done to achieve certain target behaviors or short-term goals. However, if what one is after is deep-rooted change or a shift in one's consciousness or existential way of being, then goals typically get in the way. Take the words of Alan Watts (1957), the eminent scholar of Eastern Philosophy. In his book *The Way of Zen*, he wrote:

> This is a first principle in the study of Zen and of any Far Eastern art: hurry, and all that it involves, is fatal. For there is no goal to be attained. The moment a goal is conceived it becomes impossible to practice the discipline of the art, to master the very rigor of its technique. Under the watchful and critical eye of a master one may practice the writing of Chinese characters for days and days, months and months. But he watches as a gardener watches the growth of a tree, and wants his student to have the attitude of the tree—the attitude of purposeless growth in which there are no short cuts because every stage of the way is both beginning and end. Thus the most accomplished master no more congratulates himself upon "arriving" than the most fumbling beginner.
>
> Paradoxical as it may seem, the purposeful life has no content, no point. It hurries on and on, and misses everything. Not hurrying, the purposeless life misses nothing, for it is only when there is no goal and no rush that the human senses are fully open to receive the world. Absence of hurry also involves a certain lack of interference with the natural course of events, especially when it is felt that the natural course follows principles which are not foreign to human intelligence. For, as we have seen, the Taoist mentality makes, or forces, nothing but "grows" everything. (Chapter 4, para. 5–6)

Once again it is the writers (and poets) who make the most convincing arguments. Herman Hess (2012) wrote the following in his transcendental novel *Siddhartha*:

> What could I say to you that would be of value, except that perhaps you seek too much, that as a result of your seeking you cannot find.
>
> "When someone is seeking," said Siddhartha, "It happens quite easily that he only sees the thing that he is seeking; that he is unable to find anything, unable to absorb anything, because he is only thinking of the thing he is seeking, because he has a goal, because he is obsessed with his goal. Seeking means: to have a goal; but finding means: to be free, to be receptive, to have no goal" (p. 79).

Trust the Process

What allows us to be able to let go of goals and techniques is our ability and experience of trusting the process. Such trust cannot be taught; it can only be gained through experience. I was powerfully reminded of this recently when I went snorkeling and then learned to scuba dive for the first time. I am a terrible swimmer. And I know that it is my fear of drowning that keeps me from enjoying the water and becoming an adequate swimmer. If I simply relaxed and became one with the water, the experience would become much more enjoyable. I understand all this intellectually, However, when the fear crosses so easily into terror at the level of my reptilian brain, theory goes quickly out the window. Nevertheless, the beauty and serenity of the aquatic world captivate and entice me. So I don a life jacket and go in search of beauty and adventure. After snorkeling a while, I wanted to challenge myself and began to set performance goals. The goals provided impetus and motivation but also changed the experience. Once I had a goal, it helped me to focus and disregard the other small discomforts that previously annoyed me. However, as I kept on stroking and yet did not arrive at my intended destination, the experience changed. I became obsessed with the goal and the focus shifted toward completion of the goal and why it was taking so long. My breathing became shallow and hurried. The previous discomforts became magnified. A mild panic set in. What was previously an enjoyable experience became goal oriented. Striving became driving, a driving force to complete the mission as soon as possible so I could reward myself with a gulp of unimpeded air. The irony, of course, was that sufficient air was there all along if I could learn to relax and let go. It was fine for me to set the goal as it was nice to have a destination and direction. Achieving the goal could even have enhanced my self-esteem and given me additional confidence. However, this all depended upon the process. Indeed, my confidence would surely have grown if the process and experience were enjoyable and affirming. On the other hand, when process was subsumed under achievement, panic soon set in. Though I eventually achieved my goal, my fear of water did not diminish. What mattered more in the end was not goals but process. In trusting the process, I found that if I focused simply on my breath and even counted my breaths one by one, I would eventually arrive at my destination much sooner than I thought, often without awareness; and it was much more enjoyable while consuming much less air and energy in the process.

Having enjoyed the aquatic world on the surface of the ocean, I wanted to go deeper and decided to give scuba diving a try. I was tempted to confront my terror because the tour guide shared his own experience. He said that at the beginning, he desperately did not want to submerge himself. Yet, after twenty minutes of being down, he did not want to come back up. This was exactly my experience as I once again learned to relax and trust the process—the very basic process of my breathing. The tangible proof was how much less air I consumed once I learned to trust. This allowed me to stay under for much longer. What ultimately convinced me was my own subjective experience. Mere encouragement from friends and the tour guide was grossly insufficient for me to exchange the safety of a life jacket for a heavy scuba tank. I had to go through the experience myself. And yes, everything was much more enjoyable once I relaxed and "learned" that everything was going to be okay. In fact, more than okay, for I truly did not want to come back up after learning to be one with my breath and my surroundings. Once again Watts (1957) teaches:

> But, so far as Zen is concerned, the end results have nothing to do with it. For, as we have seen all along, Zen has no goal; it is a traveling without point, with nowhere to go. To travel is to be alive, but to get somewhere is to be dead, for as our own proverb says, "To travel well is better than to arrive."
>
> . . . One must simply face the fact that Zen is all that side of life which is completely beyond our control, and which will not come to us by any amount of forcing or wrangling or cunning—

> stratagems which only produce fakes of the real thing. (excerpts, Chapter 4, para. 97–99)

Regarding letting go of goals, plans, and trusting the process, I'm reminded of a popular Christian saying: Men plan, God laughs. We think we are in charge and make plans as best we can. It behooves us to understand that there is a greater power at play. The Chinese equivalent would be the following well-known tale of a man and his horse. There was once an old man living in ancient China who bred horses for a living. One day, his best stallion ran away. People from his village came to console him for losing such a fine animal but were surprised by his equanimity and acceptance. "Is that so?" he mused? "Loss is inevitable and when something leaves, something else will eventually come along." Sure enough, a few days later, the stallion returned together with a magnificent mare. Everyone congratulated the old man for having gained another splendid horse. "Is that so?" the old man replied. "When you gain something, often something else is lost. There is no point in getting overly excited." True enough; weeks later, the old man's son broke his leg after falling off the newly acquired mare. The fall turned out to be severe to the point of crippling the son for the rest of his life. With his only son now a cripple, the villagers consoled the old man, expecting him to be shattered. "Is that so?" the old man replied stoically. "Some accidents turn into blessings in disguise." A decade later, the country was plunged into a brutal civil war. One day, one of the contending armies raided the village and forcibly conscripted all the young men, leaving behind a young man with a bad limp—the old man's son. Men plan, God laughs.

Congruence and Authenticity: Becoming Who We Are

My colleague Jason Dias (2017) wrote that our goal in supervision is not only to develop highly skilled technicians in the room but to help our supervisees become the right person such that they grow to be a healing presence to others. We train to become masters of our profession, at which point we can let go and simply be with people. Once we have become that person, we no longer need to try to help them. We help by simply being who we are. Thus, Jason often repeats the following phrase to his supervisees, "Stop trying to help and instead strive to be helpful."

So that right person is, of course, ourselves. Yet both Dias and Nietzsche point out that how can one be anyone but ourself? Nietzsche's famous aphorism to "become yourself" and "consummate your life" (as cited in Yalom, 1992) initially appears foolish but is actually quite profound. If we think about it, how can we be anyone but ourselves? Yet becoming oneself is the end point of training. We start with the examination and understanding of ourselves. We then begin the painful process of deconstructing, emptying, and changing ourselves. The end point, at last, is to return to ourselves—a self and a presence that is both the same and different from who we were. So once more we recall that famous Zen or Taoist saying about seeing the mountains and rivers once again as mountains and rivers after deconstructing them (Weixin, 1949).

This brings to mind my personal development as a therapist. As I alluded to previously, during the process of "selfing," I realized that I had been an existentialist all along. Even as a teenager I preferred hanging out under the stars, talking "nonsense" with a few close friends instead of partying. I did not realize it at the time, but I was contemplating my existence and my place in this vast universe. It was nerdy but I enjoyed it. I also recall numerous times sitting with friends as they poured their hearts out to me. It felt both slightly strange (this is not what teenagers were supposed to do) and very much at home when bearing witness to my friends' struggles. I was a neophyte and unrefined therapist who was simply doing my best to be a companion to my friends. Graduate school became a period of deconstruction of what it meant to be a healer. I was training to be a competent mental health professional who critically examined the role of a friend versus a therapist. I gained a variety of clinical skills and eventually graduated and passed my licensing exam. Now as I am well into the second half of my life, I am doing my best to once again be that friend, companion, and healing presence that I was during my teenage years. I'd like to think that I'm a better friend, companion, and healer now. But honestly, I cannot recall or assess how much of a healing presence I was to my teenage friends back then. I'm sure my friends were grateful. The process of emptying and deconstruction continues. I can only smile at the recollection of being that neophyte therapist that I didn't even know I was during my teenage years. One thing I know for certain. I now consistently listen for such "unknowing qualities" from applicants who dare to chase their dream of becoming therapists. Have their friends always regarded them as a good listener? Do they have that basic curiosity for life and their place in the cosmos? For I know that the goal of training is circular and I must have good stock if I am to help supervisees return to themselves. There must be an affinity for bearing witness and companionship, and I believe it must be innate. The applicant/supervisee may or may not yet recognize this quality within. But upon reflection, they too will begin to realize that their friends recognized their gift for they were often sought out for healing.

Zhuangzi (2006) also recognized that there must be a host with an affinity for receiving the Tao. He wrote:

> If the Tao could be served up, everyone would serve it up to their lords. If the Tao could be offered, there is no one who would not offer it to their parents. If the Tao could be spoken of, there is no one who would not speak of it to their brothers and sisters. If the Tao could be passed on, there is no one who would not pass it on to their heirs. However, it obviously cannot be so and the reason is as follows.
>
> > If there is no true centre within to receive it, it cannot remain;
> > if there is no true direction outside to guide it, it cannot be received.
> > If the true centre is not brought out it cannot receive on the outside.
> > The sage cannot draw it forth.
> > If what comes in from the outside is not welcomed by the true centre,
> > then the sage cannot let it go.
> > Fame is something sought by all,
> > but don't go for too much of it.
> > Benevolence and righteousness are as the houses of the former kings,
> > useful for one night's shelter,
> > but don't stay there too long.
> > To stay long causes considerable adverse comment.
> > (Chapter 14, para. 34)

Lao Tzu also recognized that the affinity for the Tao, like the gift for healing and companionship, will often seem strange to others. Yet those who understand will immediately begin to put it into practice.

Tao Te Ching, Verse 41 (excerpts)

When a superior man hears of the Tao,
he immediately begins to embody it.

When an average man hears of the Tao,
he half believes it, half doubts it.
When a foolish man hears of the Tao,
he laughs out loud.
If he didn't laugh,
it wouldn't be the Tao. (Lao Tzu, 1995)

Zhuangzi (1998) understood the same circular principle when he wrote the following Parable of the Old Swimmer:

> Confucius was observing the cataract at Spinebridge where the water fell from a height of thirty fathoms and the mist swirled for forty tricents. No tortoise, alligator, fish, or turtle could swim there. Spotting an older man swimming in the water, Confucius thought that he must have suffered some misfortune and wished to die. So he had his disciples line up along the current to rescue the man. But after the man had gone several hundred yards he came out by himself. With disheveled hair, he was walking along singing and enjoying himself beneath the embankment.
>
> Confucius followed after the man and inquired of him, saying, "I thought you were a ghost, but when I looked more closely I saw that you are a man. May I ask if you have a special way for treading water?"
>
> "No, I have no special way. I began with what was innate, grew up with my nature, and completed my destiny. I enter the very center of the whirlpools and emerge as a companion of the torrents. I follow along with the way of the water and do not impose myself on it. That's how I do my treading."
>
> "What do you mean by 'begin with what was innate, grew up with your nature, and completed your destiny'?" asked Confucius.
>
> "I was born among these hills and feel secure among them —that's what's innate. I grew up in the water and feel secure in it—that's my nature. I do not know why I am like this, yet that's how I am—that's my destiny." (p. 182)

The Importance of Fundamentals

Ving's decision to become a roaster and understand the coffee beans from its source taught me about the importance of mastering fundamentals and returning to the origin. After learning about Ving's decision, my friend Evone pointed out to me the beautiful paradox in Ving's decision to "move forward by returning to the past/origin." Exactly right, I thought to myself! This immediately reminded me of the vital importance of the basics and fundamentals when it comes to the practice of psychotherapy. In teaching how to conduct therapy informed by the existential–humanistic approach that de-emphasizes techniques, I'm often faced with the question of what to teach and demonstrate to my supervisees. When pondering this, I think back to a few things that my ballroom dance instructor taught me regarding how it was that the professional dancers that I admire so much were able to make something so beautiful but difficult look so easy. This was exactly what I observed as Ving was preparing my cup of *Homey Latte.* She worked quickly and efficiently while chatting with me. A cup of delicious latte materialized before me after three minutes of expert ministrations. It was so smooth that I took it for granted. And it was only later, as she was describing to me the importance of the various steps of brewing a good cup of coffee, that I realized how each of Ving's steps was over-learned, the result of daily practice. It was a wonderful demonstration of Wu Wei discussed throughout this book. Ving's smooth and well-practiced motions reminded me of the popular Chinese aphorism: "Ten minutes of on-stage performance, ten years of off-stage toil."

In the spirit of Wu Wei, my ballroom dance teacher encouraged me to continue to work on the basics and the fundamental of dance and not be so overly enamored with all the complicated dance steps. She told me that she, too, was astonished to see the world champions working daily on their fundamentals. If world champions are working to improve their fundamentals, how about you? For without proper fundamentals, I would not be able to dance those beautiful steps. The best I could do was an ungainly imitation, which my teacher did not have the heart to tell me was not pleasing to the eye. I finally confronted this sad reality when reviewing my own dance videos. Fantasy painfully dashed at the feet of cold reality. I did not tell my teacher at the time, but she probably knew anyway how "boring" the fundamentals were to me. I wanted to move on to the advanced steps because they looked more interesting, beautiful, and fun. I was not ready to appreciate the simplistic beauty inherent in the important subtleties to be found in each fundamental step. I was unable to appreciate the joys to be found in having the fundamentals become a more natural inner part of my basic body movement. I had not learned what it was to dance from the inside out, rather than outside in. It is a process I must sustain and break through if I am fascinated enough with dance. I am still on that journey of discovery and experience.

The same is true of psychotherapy and life. The simple things are the most difficult. We must stick with it until the difficult once again become more simplistic. Ving and my dance teachers confirmed for me that the important aspects of therapy are a way of life, not just confined to professional practice. They also helped to strengthen my conviction of teaching and demonstrating to my students the importance of learning and over-learning the basic "micro-skills" that are essential to facilitating therapeutic change. It reinforced for me that attentive listening, empathy, authenticity are not the basics that we learn and move forward from, but critical fundamentals that we return to over and over again. For example, when lecturing about empathy, Carl Rogers (1980) stated that his goal was not to "empathize" with his clients. Instead, what Rogers strived for was simply to understand his client as best he could. He taught about empathy as a way of being rather than a particular skill to master. Sounds easy doesn't it, something as simple as understanding another?

Finally, all of this was illustrated to me in the commencement speech given by Admiral William McRaven, to the graduates of the University of Texas in 2014. McRaven taught the graduates that it was okay to be a "sugar cookie." A sugar cookie was someone who failed some form of inspection during SEAL training and was ordered to run fully clothed into the ocean and then roll around on the beach until every part of their body was covered with sand. "Sometimes no matter how well you prepare or how well you perform you still end up as a sugar cookie," McRaven said. "It's just the way life is sometimes." Through the example of the simple and seemingly unrelated mundane task of making one's bed, McRaven then spoke about the importance of getting back to the fundamentals and doing the little things right:

> Every morning in basic SEAL training, my instructors, who at the time were all Vietnam veterans, would show up in my barracks room, and the first thing they would inspect was your bed.
>
> If you did it right, the corners would be square, the covers pulled tight, the pillow centered just under the headboard, and the extra blanket folded neatly at the foot of the rack. Rack—that's Navy talk for bed.
>
> It was a simple task, mundane at best. But every morning we were required to make our beds to perfection. It seemed a little

> ridiculous at the time, particularly in light of the fact that we were aspiring to be real warriors, tough battle-hardened SEALs. But the wisdom of this simple act has been proven to me many times over.
>
> If you make your bed every morning you will have accomplished the first task of the day. It will give you a small sense of pride, and it will encourage you to do another task and another and another.
>
> By the end of the day, that one task completed will have turned into many tasks completed. Making your bed will also reinforce the fact that little things in life matter. If you can't do the little things right, you will never do the big things right.
>
> And, if by chance you have a miserable day, you will come home to a bed that is made—that you made—and a made bed gives you encouragement that tomorrow will be better. If you want to change the world, start off by making your bed. (Jacobs, 2015)

Admiral McRaven organized the raid that killed Osama Bin Laden. His lessons about life and leadership encourage me to stay with the fundamentals and pass that lesson onto my supervisees if we desire to dance and practice psychotherapy from the inside out.

Wu Wei (無爲/无为)

Paradoxically, one of the most difficult things that supervisees need to let go of is their desire to help or fix their clients. This is not to be confused with being unmotivated or not caring about their clients. It has more to do with supervisees getting out of their own way and/or getting out of their clients' way on the path to healing. It is about being intentionally non-intentional and willfully without will, choosing deliberate non-action or effortless action, and acting without premeditation. In other words, it's about the Taoist concept of Wu Wei. Other ways of understanding Wu Wei is intention and act being simultaneous, not forcing, not imposing, not interfering. Wu Wei has been described as non-doing, but it is not doing nothing. Zhuangzi (2013) described the mind of Wu Wei as flowing like water, still like a mirror, and responding like an echo.

> When a man does not dwell in self, then things will of themselves reveal their forms to him. His movement is like that of water, his stillness like that of a mirror, his responses like those of an echo. Blank eyed, he seems to be lost; motionless, he has the limpidity of water. Because he is one with it, he achieves harmony; should he reach out for it, he would lose it. Never does he go ahead of other men, but always follows in their wake. (Chapter 33, para. 30)

How can we teach our supervisees about non-intentional intentionality? How do we teach them to be intentionally non-intentional? Alan Watts (1957) wrote of the same challenge and suggested that we learn from the Japanese Zen practices of archery and calligraphy. He described Eugene Herrigel's experience of grasping the art of archery from a Japanese Zen Master and learning from the Japanese Zen Master Sabro Hasegawa how the process of painting with a brush can be understood as a "controlled accident." Herrigel spent five years learning how to release the bowstring unintentionally, the same way a ripe fruit bursts its skin. He was learning to resolve the paradox of unintentional intention and effortless effort, trying to figure out how to release the arrow wu-hsin, without mind, and wu-nien, without choice. His master asked him to keep working and practicing relentlessly, yet without trying and making an effort at the same time. To eventually get to the point in which the arrow shoots itself. Through years of this Wu Wei form of practice, the arrow indeed shot itself one day, yet Herrigel never understood why. It was the same principle as calligraphy or learning to paint with a brush. The brush must draw by itself. And this comes about only through endless practice, but the type of practice that comes without making an effort. The writing or painting happens wu-hsin and wu-nien, just the same as in swordsmanship. For one must thrust without deciding to thrust because there is no time to decide. Decision and action must be simultaneous. These are apt metaphors for the supervisory and therapy process for we, too, are striving to teach our supervisees about unintentional intentionality and how "evenly hovering attention" in psychotherapy is discipline in spontaneity and spontaneity in discipline.

As Alan Watts (1957) suggests, non-intentioned intentionality can only be achieved through endless practice and experience. Both the continuing story of Ving and the following two parables from Zhuangzi below illustrate the same point while emphasizing the skill of focusing. Wu Wei must be grasped experientially. An intellectual understanding is only the beginning. In other words, there is no substitute for accumulating clinical hours and lived experience. Our supervisees must put in the practice time. What we can provide as supervisors is not only the how-to of clinical skills but also the experiential learning of what it feels like to experience Wu Wei or the Tao. In the meantime, we must continually urge our supervisees to keep on practicing with the faith that their persistence will pay off one day when the fruit reaches its time to separate itself from the tree. Both the supervisor and supervisee practice by faith without knowing when that day will come or even how the arrow begins to "shoot itself."

Ving taught me this as she described how she acquired the skill to become a barista. Ving told me that she traveled to Taiwan to learn the techniques and know-how of what it took to become a good barista. However, that was just the beginning. She went further to state that she would not hesitate to pass on her knowledge, recipes, and techniques to me if I were interested in becoming a barista. However, this would not turn me into a barista. So what would I need to do then I asked? Ving explained to me that she learned the knowledge of what it took to operate a café and brew cups of good coffee from her apprenticeship in Taiwan. However, what helped her to become the barista she is today was practice. There is no substitute for practice—endless focused practice followed by the mindful tasting and critique of one's work. I can teach you about water temperature, timing, how to grind and pack the beans. However, what I cannot pass on to you is the feel and intuition required in the art of brewing a good cup of coffee. That you must learn on your own by constantly brewing and tasting endless cups of coffee. Take the simple act of even-pouring to extract the flavor from your beans. I can show you the technique, but one must practice to get the feel of the pour that makes the critical subtle difference in a good cup of coffee. The same principles apply in the important steps of packing the coffee grounds. As you can imagine, the density of the packed coffee grounds will impact the rate of the hot water flow, which in turn impacts the taste of the coffee. There are presses that will allow one to adjust the tension of the press. Uniformity and objectivity! However, experienced baristas prefer simple presses because it is important for them to develop their own feel for the press and thus better control the tension of each press. "If you do it enough, it becomes second nature and you learn to adjust on the fly" Ving explained. The science of the water temperature, coffee grind, and press tension are important. But it is the art of the human touch and intuition that decides the subtleties of a good cup of coffee. And this art can only be achieved with practice.

It takes about two to three minutes to brew a cup of coffee. Numerous important steps are packed into this short interval of time. Thus, one must be focused in order to execute the required step at the required time for the necessary period of time. Even though the time interval is short, one must not rush. It is the paradoxical act of waiting in anticipation. All of this reflects the spirit of Zen and the Taoist concept of Wu Wei. One must be intentional in one's practice and yet the paradoxical goal of all this practice is to be able to execute unintentionally.

Herrigel's intentioned non-intentionality reminds me of why Ving is continuing on her journey of becoming a better barista. She cannot explain exactly how her skills have improved as a barista. She cannot explain exactly the feel of the even pour or the right tension for pressing the coffee grounds. She knows that she has improved, but she also knows that she must continue to learn and practice if she is to continue improving. Herrigel spent five years to achieve the feel of the arrow shooting itself. He cannot explain how or why it happened. It just did. He came to the point in which he can really begin. I can't help but think that perhaps this is the same with Ving. After seven years, she came to a point at which she can also really begin to attain the unattainable. It is the same with me and dancing. Through numerous lessons and hearing (oftentimes without understanding) how one must dance from the inside out, I finally was able to occasionally feel and experience what my teachers were trying to communicate to me. And this is what I'm trying to achieve with my students. I, too, urge them to paradoxically keep on working and working but also to let go of their desire to change their clients and "trust the process." My moment of such awakening happened serendipitously during internship when I heard myself utter a phrase similar to Winston, my graduate school mentor, without even trying. The words just flowed through my mouth. I was stunned! It was like an out-of-body experience. I had internalized my mentor without deliberate effort and intention. It just happened—ironically enough, after I left him for internship. Listening to Ving, reading and educating myself regarding Wu Wei and Zen, and my own dedication to practice helped me to learn and teach about the paradox of intentional non-intentionality. Ving's dedication to her art inspires me to similarly dedicate myself to my own pursuit of becoming a better trainer and therapist.

Finally, my conversation with Ving takes place in the context of Ving's soon-to-close café. Behind the counter stands Christine, Ving's apprentice. After a year of working under Ving, Christine has plans of returning to her hometown to open her own café! My friend Evone tells me that Christine has improved as a barista after brewing and tasting countless cups of coffee herself. So Ving's work and dedication ripple on through Christine, who is also intentionally traveling along her own path of pursuing the art of the unintentional.

Zhuangzi (1998) also understood that certain skills cannot be passed on in books and must be learned experientially. For example, he wrote the following parable to warn us of the limitation of book knowledge:

> Duke Huan was reading in the upper part of his hall and Wheelwright Flat was hewing a wheel in the lower part. Setting aside his hammer and chisel, the wheelwright went to the upper part of the hall and inquired of Duke Huan, saying, "I venture to ask what words Your Highness is reading?"
>
> "The words of sages," said the duke.
>
> "Are the sages still alive?"
>
> "They're already dead," said the duke.
>
> "Then what my lord is reading are merely the dregs of the ancients."
>
> "How can you, a wheelwright, comment upon what I am reading?" ask Duke Huan. "if you can explain yourself, all right. If you cannot explain yourself, you shall die."
>
> "I look at it from my own occupation," said Wheelwright Flat. "If the spokes are loose, they'll fit sweet as a whistle but the wheel won't be solid. If they're too tight, you won't be able to insert them no matter how hard you try. To make them neither too loose nor too tight is something you sense in your hand and feel in your heart. There's a knack to it that can't be put in words. I haven't been able to teach it to my son, and my son hasn't been able to learn it from me. That's why I'm still hewing wheels after seventy years. When they died, the ancients took with them what they couldn't transmit. So what you are reading are the dregs of the ancients." (pp. 128–29)

Focusing

Zhuangzi (1998) wrote about the spirit of Wu Wei and the concept of focusing when he told the story of The Cicada Catcher (Chapter 19), which was presented earlier in this book in the chapter on Humanistic Education. Eugene Gendlin (1981), a student and later colleague of Carl

Rogers, wrote extensively about focusing. Focusing begins by quieting the mind. The best way to quiet the mind is not by criticizing or arguing with it. Fighting with your mind is useless. Instead, Timothy Galloway (1997), who applied the principles of focusing and Wu Wei to the game of tennis, taught that the way to deepen concentration through sight is to focus on subtle details, something not easily perceived, such as the patterns made by the seams of a tennis ball as it spins. Teaching players to focus on such details is much more worthwhile than asking them to just "watch the ball." When we begin focusing on such subtle details, a strange thing begins to happen. We begin to develop more interest. We begin to discover that there is so much more to know about something than we thought we already knew. Once again, this un-knowing is a powerful principle of focus. And it is such interest that helps us to maintain that focus for an extended period of time.

Consciousness can be compared to a light shining in a dark forest. By virtue of this light, we will be able to see within a certain radius, and the closer the object is to the light, the more detail will be revealed because of the illumination. We can turn this light into a searchlight if we focus the beams through a reflector. All the light beams are focused in one direction, and this is the power of focused attention. Objects that were previously lost in darkness can be shown with greater clarity when they are brought into the path of the searchlight. On the other hand, if the lens of the searchlight were dirty, or imperfections were present in the reflector, or the light beams started oscillating, the beam would then be dispersed and the quality of the focus would be diminished. Distraction is the imperfections or the dirt on the lens degrading the quality of the illumination. The light of consciousness can be focused upon external materials or internal thoughts or feelings. Indeed, focusing on the cicada's wings is what allowed the cicada catcher to succeed.

Finally, the following Zhuangzi passage regarding action and non-action as introduced by the Catholic theologian Thomas Merton (2010) poetically summarizes the concept of Wu Wei:

> The non-action of the wise man is not inaction.
> It is not studied. It is not shaken by anything.
> The sage is quiet because he is not moved,
> Not because he *wills* to be quiet.
> Still water is like glass.
> You can look in it and see the bristles on your chin.
> It is a perfect level;

A carpenter could use it.
If water is so clear, so level,
How much more the spirit of man?
The heart of the wise man is tranquil.
It is the mirror of heaven and earth
The glass of everything.
Emptiness, stillness, tranquility, tastelessness,
Silence, non-action: this is the level of heaven and earth.
This is perfect Tao. Wise men find here
Their resting place.
Resting, they are empty.

From emptiness comes the unconditioned.
From this, the conditioned, the individual things.
So from the sage's emptiness, stillness arises:
From stillness, action. From action, attainment.
From their stillness comes their non-action, which is also action
For stillness is joy. Joy is free from care
Fruitful in long years.
Joy does all things without concern:
For emptiness, stillness, tranquility, tastelessness,
Silence, and non-action
Are the root of all things. (pp. 80–81)

Nietzsche (2008) wrote, "Slow is the experience of all deep wells: long must they wait before they know what fell into their depth" (p. 46). Experienced therapists will know that it is the stillness and tranquility of the group leader that overcomes the group's agitation. The leader's stillness and consciousness are the primary tools. Group psychotherapist John Heider (2005) understood this well:

> Imagine that there is a pond in this valley. When no fears or desires stir the surface of the pond, the water forms a perfect mirror. In this mirror, you can see the reflection of Tao. You can see God and you can see creation.
>
> Go into the valley, and be still, and watch the pond. Go as often as you wish. Your silence will grow. The pond will never run dry. The valley, the pond, and Tao are all within you. (p. 11)

> The leader teaches more through being than through doing. The quality of one's silence conveys more than long speeches.
>
> Be still follow your inner wisdom. In order to know your inner wisdom, you have to be still.
>
> The leader who knows how to be still and feel deeply will probably be effective. But the leader who chatters and boasts and tries to impress the group has no center and carries little weight. (p. 45)
>
> The leader's stillness overcomes the group's agitation. The leader's consciousness is the primary tool of this work. (p. 89)

Structure and Flow

I recall supervising a student in Hong Kong who had to present a treatment plan for a group she was running. Working in a more evidenced-based setting, she was asked to plan out an eight-week treatment plan with stages and goals for each meeting. Furthermore, she was asked to structure discrete times planned for the warm-up, working, wrap-up, and conclusion periods of each group. This was structure, and it was about prediction and control. On the other hand, following the ways of Wu Wei, it appears that there is no structure at all. Everything goes with the flow. How unpredictable and frightening for a novice therapist in training.

However, what I endeavor to explain to all of my supervisees is that following Wu Wei and working existentially does not mean there is no structure. I explain that it's understandable to plan and structure the group initially when one is learning the craft. This is done to alleviate our own anxiety as much as the client's. However, as one becomes more comfortable as a therapist, one can begin to let go of some of that control and manifest structure and begin to attune and align oneself with a greater and much more powerful underlying structure that the sages understood as the way of the Tao. Zhuangzi (2006) wrote:

> Fish enjoy water, humans enjoy the Tao. Enjoying water, the fish stick to the pond and find all they need to survive there. Enjoying the Tao, people do nothing and their lives are fulfilled. The saying goes that fish forget about each other in the pond and people forget each other in the Tao. (Chapter 6, para. 40)

Conversely, Zhuangzi (1998) warns us about going against the grain and not following the flow through the following parable:

> Don't you know about the praying mantis? Angrily waving its arms, it blocks the path of an onrushing chariot, not realizing that the task is far beyond it. This is because it puts a high premium on its own ability. Be restrained and cautious. If you put a high premium on always bragging about yourself and thereby offend him, you will be in jeopardy.
>
> And don't' you know about the tiger keeper? He dares not give a live animal to his charges, for fear of stirring up their fury when they kill it, nor dares he give them a whole animal, for fear of stirring up their fury when they tear it apart. By gauging the times when the tigers are hungry or full, he can fathom their fury. Although the tigers are of a different species from man, they try to please their keeper because he goes along with them, whereas they kill those who go against them.
>
> "He who loves horses catches their dung in baskets and receives their urine in giant clam shells. But if a mosquito or a snipefly should alight upon one of his horses and he slaps it at the wrong moment, the horse will chomp through its bit, break his head, and smash his chest. His intentions are the best, yet he may perish through his love. Can one afford not to be cautious? (pp. 36–37, excerpts)

Underlying structures are more about principles, metaphors, and paradoxes rather than tangible facts, plans, and logic. They concern themselves more with the needs of the group at the moment rather than adherence to a preset plan. All of this is beautifully illustrated by a colleague of mine, Dave Schulkin, an existential therapist and avid surfer. Man-made structures such as roller coasters, race cars, and even acrobatic stunt airplanes can provide great excitement, allowing us to be in control right up to the edge. Contrast that with the beauty, power, duration, and excitement of riding a wave. While the former is predictable and within our control, important elements of life experience are missing when compared to surrendering ourselves to the natural flow of the waves. What are these important elements of life and therapy? They include waiting and reading, focusing and sensing, timing and positioning, rhythm and pacing, energy and flow, presence and awareness, transience and temporality, nature and humanity. While most of these elements are also present when riding a rollercoaster, driving a race car, and flying a stunt plane, they are experienced differently when the force of propulsion that we are tapping into is that of nature itself. With the energy of the waves, it's infinitely more powerful, everlasting, unpredictable, beautiful, and at times even awe-inspiring. Once one has "caught the wave" and experienced this great transformative power, one is unlikely to return to the manifest structures that, while effective, pale in comparison to the Way of the Tao. Consider the beautifully descriptive words of my colleague Dave in his book chapter, A Journey Toward Authenticity:

> I dip my hands into the cold water, feeling it pass through my fingers as I use its resistance to propel myself forward. My arms, used to knowing what to do after more than 20 years of surfing, get me from the edge of the shore, past the turbulent rows of white water, out to the lineup, where I want to be. There I wait, and feel the level of the ocean rise and fall in a rhythm much slower than my everyday pace of life. I contemplate the waves of energy that are moving through the sea and pause to consider which one I would like to attempt to flow with. Timing and positioning are critical.
>
> In a last-minute decision, I turn and paddle my surfboard toward the shore. As the energy catches up with me, I can feel the wave lift me up and thrust me forward. Now I am part of the wave, moving with an ever-changing wall of water. The board under my feet feels like an extension of my body as I fluidly turn and adapt to the constantly shifting environment. Swiftly swooping on the surface of the water, I intuitively make split-second decisions and micro-adjustments to stay attuned to the most powerful part of the wave. I am fully aware and present in order to flow with my surroundings, but also because I know these fleeting moments where I am actually riding the wave will not last forever. Soon the energy dissipates and I use the last remaining speed I have to turn off the back of the wave and coast to a stop in calm water. My union with the wave has passed. I am once more a human being on a board, paddling back out to the lineup to get into the best position to catch the next wave that rolls my way. . . .
>
> Embracing authenticity is an act of embracing uncertainty. There is no way of knowing exactly what is going to happen or what the next moment will bring. I can only observe what is happening right now and make choices based on those observations. As a lifelong surfer, I can't help but relate this directly to my experiences in the ocean. When I first catch a

> wave, I have an idea of what that wave might do, but the reality is I don't really know. So when I am riding a wave, I am living fully, using my intuition and interacting with what is happening in the moment, just as the existential–humanistic model encourages me to seize the present-moment and make the most of what I have right now, since it is all there is.
>
> And that is ultimately the goal: to have that awareness and presence both within and without, to be present with our existential givens. (Schulkin, 2014, pp. 140–141)

The process is certainly not safe and predictable. Yet when one is willing to trust the process and tap into the great force of nature, unforgettable transformative experiences are likely to ensue. This is what is meant by respect for natural laws and recognizing that the ultimate authority rests with nature. For the goal of psychotherapy practiced from an existential–humanistic perspective is to align oneself with that underlying natural order.

Take for example the concept of structure and frame within psychotherapy. Psychodynamic therapy emphasizes strong boundaries and a firm analytic frame. A mature and disciplined therapist is one who is able to hold fast to his or her boundaries and establish that strong and secure frame for much can be revealed if one is able to maintain one's analytic frame. For example, if one can establish a strong boundary regarding the ending time of therapy, one can gain helpful information about the underlying, unconscious dynamics of the client. Humanistic therapists, on the other hand, adopt a different view of boundaries and time. Instead of strict adherence to an artificial frame, humanistic therapists tend to be more flexible with their boundaries while seeking to align themselves with the natural structure and frame of life.

Humanistic therapists will argue that the same interpersonal dynamics can still be explored at the end of therapy without such a strict boundary surrounding time. Endings are inevitable and evocative enough in the natural order of things. Waves will come and go. There are natural rhythms to the process of life and therapy. Spring follows after winter, the timing of which is not in our control. The end of the therapy session is viewed as a natural part of the therapeutic process and will be experienced one way or another. The difference is, to what extent is the ending artificial, and to what extent is it more part of a flow? The vagaries of life are cruel (and lovely) enough without us accentuating them artificially. What is required of us is to increase our awareness and align ourselves with the underlying natural process as opposed to creating an overly rigid artificial frame. This does not mean that sessions end at the whim of the therapist or client, although sometimes that may be the case. Structures are necessary to help us manage our lives. What humanistic psychologists advocate for is boundaries that are flexible, natural, and humane. Endings are difficult enough as it is. Therapists and clients can deal with such limitations without the need to artificially enhance the experience. Nature is fine the way it is. It would behoove us to surrender and align ourselves with its wisdom and awesome power.

Similarly, psychodynamic therapy and humanistic psychotherapy both take seriously the concept of authority and our relationship to it, though each takes a very different approach. Psychodynamic therapists are more likely to analyze one's relationship with important authority figures in our lives. Humanistic therapists, on the other hand, take on a more deferential attitude toward authority, preferring to locate authority within transpersonal elements of nature. One approach emphasizes transference and analysis, the other advocates surrender and awe.

Not Mastery but Surrender

The advanced lesson beyond letting go is learning to surrender. For me, surrender was originally filled with negative connotations associated mainly with failure, submission, or defeat. With such thoughts, I naturally detested the counsel of surrendering ourselves to God. It often felt like the dominant commandment given by a master to a slave, devoid of love, respect, or awe. Surrender was experienced as humility and shame. The God to be worshipped felt like an insecure tyrant who required our submission. The spiritual language regarding surrender mainly consisted of power and majesty. Surrendering required coercion. Of course, this was an immensely distorted concept of God, yet one that was influenced by much of my experience. Such spiritual experiences have their natural parallels to supervision and therapy when they are practiced in a distant, hierarchical manner.

On the other hand, for Taoist philosophers the weak, the submissive, and the useless are preferable in some ways to the strong, the dominant, and the useful. Zhuangzi employed the themes of a useless stinktree, an empty boat, and a turtle dragging its tail in the mud, while Lao Tzu extolled the virtue of darkness, the softly yielding power of water, and the lowliness and receptivity of the ocean. Some have characterized the

Taoist approach as more representative of feminine energy. Viewed in this way, the goal of supervision does not become the mastery of skills along the lines of achievement and conquest, but rather more a matter of attunement, alignment, and reverence. It is the recognition that the art of therapy is much too profound to be mastered. There are no master clinicians. We are all on the path of learning. There is nothing to be conquered for when we climb, it is the mountain as much as our legs that lifts us upwards. Ed Viesturs (2007), who has climbed all 14 of the 8,000-meter peaks in the world without supplemental oxygen, learned about such humility and respect from the Sherpas, who taught him to tread lightly and gently while climbing these magnificent peaks. We can only take what the mountains give us. In therapy, we must have patience and be prepared, then our clients, like the mountains, will permit us to reach their highest peaks. If we indeed have learned to "trust the process," we'd recognize that it is the process that is the master and that there is a force greater than oneself at work. Consider the painting of a woman dressed in blue hovering over a chessboard. Above the painting written in large letters is the word 'CHECKMATE." Below the painting printed in smaller letters is the following question, "What is the difference between your experience of existence and that of a saint?" The answer to that question is provided by Hafiz (2006), a Persian mystic poet from the thirteenth century who wrote a poem titled "Tripping with Joy," in which he describes playing chess with God. According to Hafiz, the difference between us and the saint is that the saint trips over with joy as she surrenders to being checkmated by God, whereas we still think we have a thousand serious moves left.

Strong and Weak Therapy

Awakening our supervisees to the joy of surrendering to the ways of the Tao has to do with teaching them about practicing *weak* therapy. My colleague and good friend Todd Dubose (personal communication, April 28, 2016) contrasted strong and weak therapy in the following manner, based on the concepts of weak thought and weak theology in the works of Gianni Vattimo and Pier Aldo Rovatti (2013) and John Caputo (2006).

Weak Thought	Strong Thought
Gives primacy to the question	Privileges answers
Is relative and flexible	Is fixed and absolute
Unknowing/uncertainty are normal	Unknowing/uncertainty are flaws
Releases control	Predicts and aims for control
Truth is relative, many "truths"	Truth is absolute
The Other as welcomed stranger	The Other is a threat to sameness

Comparable to strong thought, strong therapy fixes, cures, corrects, purifies, engineers, resolves, manages, reconditions, prescribes, and directs. Depression is cured by raising serotonin levels or altering maladaptive thinking. Anger is managed through behavioral reconditioning. Inappropriate behavior is engineered into appropriate behavior. Symptoms are eliminated. Persons are orchestrated. It is a therapeutic process of certainty, knowing, and conclusiveness. Dubose proposes:

> An alternate view of therapeutic space, or a "weak therapy," that is unpredictable, uncontrollable, unknowable, egalitarian, vulnerable, accessible, relative, particular, contextual, fluid and uncertain, where Nothing and no One is Sovereign and where everyone involved is "put into play" by "the event" of caring for another human being. "Weak therapy" releases, opens, risks, fluctuates, explores, collaborates, uncovers, discloses, and unfolds; it is a therapeutic process of "perhaps," and "what might be." From this perspective, symptoms are not viewed as pathogens to eliminate but are disclosures of meaning and passion.
>
> Here, we let the fists speak, yet privilege neither violence nor peace. We provide space to hear the cry of anxiety in the wilderness, without tranquilizing it. We clarify the significance of shooting heroin, without prescribing sobriety. We sit vigil with a child's sadness of a broken toy with no less respect as we would for an adult suffering from complex trauma. Any behavior, thought or feeling is seen as unique, contextualized and radically validated. There is no ideal form of health, well-being, or the good life, just a multiplicity of incomparable expressions of Life that cannot be objectified, classified, or categorized. Change occurs without focusing on change, and power is experienced without force. The goal, being, an engaged

> understanding of lived meaning, even if such an understanding calls us to understand someone who does not want to be understood. It is a ground-less practice based on another kind of evidence that is unconditional, invisible, insubstantial, and immeasurable, though intimate and ubiquitous: purpose, love, hope, faith, wonder, in short, *lived meaning.* What is real is *existentially* significant, and the Truth is that there is no Truth—only a diversity of lived meanings. It is a place of inclusive hospitality, even for the exclusive one. It is an egalitarian openness, even for the one who is hierarchically absolute. It is a both/and world, a sharing of common existence, yet a shared existence where difference is relative though resolutely engaged. Its consolation grants no certainties, no assured solutions, no everlasting moment, but only the blessed and dangerous possibility in each lived situation of remaining the same or being otherwise—either decision, though, being received, understood, and respected. The therapist does not "treat" the "patient," but is another fellow human being mutually exploring the human condition. Here, radical understanding is not a prelude to the real therapy but is transformative in itself. Here, love need not be earned as it is freely given.

Weak Therapy	**Strong Therapy**
Explores	Fixes
Attends	Cures
Understands	Corrects
Allows	Prescribes
Invites	Directs
Change without forcing change	Change: reduce target symptoms
Therapeutic space: Khora	Therapeutic space: Clinical
Egalitarian, inclusive, relative	Rank-ordered measured comparisons

Naturally, Taoist practitioners align themselves with the practice of weak therapy. And if we are to supervise in the same way, we would create a supervisory space that is characterized by Khora, an ancient Greek term used by Plato to designate a receptacle. Plato's characterized Khora as neither being or non-being, but an interval in-between. It receives all, gives space, and has maternal overtones (womb). In this space characterized by Khora, we would give primacy to questions instead of privileging answers. The supervision would be relative and flexible, where unknowing and uncertainty are experienced as the norm rather than flaws. The supervisor would model all of this by himself or herself, surrendering to the process and releasing control. Instead of fixing the supervisee's shortcomings, both the supervisor and supervisee would together explore the supervisee's struggles, allowing the process to unfold and seeking understanding rather than prescribing correction. Khora would make room for mistakes, imperfections, anxiety, pain, and transformation. Most important, weak therapy must be embodied for the supervisee. Just as it is with lived meaning, the supervision must be alive and the embodied concepts lived out. Mere instruction is simply not enough.

Emptiness

As the passage above suggests, the process of letting go is the process of emptying, a major theme within Taoist thought. To be open and attuned to our clients, we must enter a state of emptiness in which we let go of our preconceived notions and adopt more of what the Buddhists refer to as the "beginner's mind." It is also the concept of bracketing, one of the foundational steps of phenomenology. Through bracketing, the therapist endeavors to suspend all beliefs, personal and theoretical biases, previous knowledge, judgments, expectations, and assumptions in an effort to receive the client with as much curiosity, openness, and disciplined naivete as possible even though it is impossible to achieve this completely (Spinelli, 2005).

Zhuangzi (1998) extolled the virtue of emptiness when he wrote the following parable:

> Thus he who possesses others is tied down with troubles and he who is possessed by other is best by worries. Hence Yao neither possessed men nor was he possessed by them. I would have your lordship throw off the ties that troubles you, get rid of the worries that best you, and wonder alone with the Way in the land of great Nothingness.
>
> "If someone is crossing a river in a double-hulled vessel and an empty hull comes and strikes against it, even though he may be a quick-tempered person, he will not be angry. But if there is a person in the boat, he will shout to him to steer clear. If his first shout goes unheeded, he will shout again. If the second shout goes unheeded, he will shout a third time, and that will

> certainly be followed by a stream of abuse. In the previous instance he did not get angry but in the present instance he is angry, because the previous boat was empty but this one has a person in it. If a person can empty himself and go wandering in the world, who can harm him?" (pp. 189–190)

Christopher Knight was known as the last true hermit for living alone in the woods of Maine in America for 27 years without having a conversation with another individual. When asked what motivated him to live alone for such a long time, he quoted Octavio Paz, Mexican poet and Nobel laureate, "Solitude is the profoundest fact of the human condition" and the Austro-German poet Rainer Maria Rilke, "Ultimately and precisely in the deepest and most important matters, we are unspeakably alone" (as cited in Finkel, 2017, p. 190). Perhaps Knight was simply seeking the freedom and solitude that comes from emptying oneself, becoming an empty boat. Knight found that:

> "Solitude increased my perception. But here's the tricky thing: when I applied my increased perception to myself, I lost my identity. There was no audience, no one to perform for. There was no need to define myself. I became irrelevant."
>
> The dividing line between himself and the forest, Knight said, seemed to dissolve. His isolation felt like a communion. "My desires dropped away. I didn't long for anything. I didn't even have a name. To put it romantically, I was completely free."
> . . ."I become a transparent eyeball," wrote Ralph Waldo Emerson in 'Nature.' "I am nothing, I see all."
> . . .Merton wrote that "the true solitary does not seek himself, but loses himself." (as cited in Finkel, 2017, pp. 142–143)

Emptiness was Siddhartha's goal as well: "Siddhartha has one single goal—to become empty, to become empty of thirst, desire, dreams, pleasure, and sorrow—to let the Self die. No longer to be Self, to experience the peace of an emptied heart, to experience pure thought—that was his goal" (Hess, 2012, p. 7).

Rollo May (1981), too, extolled the value of stillness and emptiness when he wrote of the importance of the pause in his book *Freedom and Destiny*. He points out that between stimulus and response is the pause: "We find Einstein remarking that 'the intervals between the events are more significant than the events themselves.' *The significance of the pause is that the rigid chain of cause and effect is broken*" (italics in the original, p. 167). The ability to pause, to will, to choose, is the essence of existence. This is what differentiates us from simpler life forms. As Victor Frankl (1985) emphasized, what determines man are not conditions but decisions, and these decisions are made during the pause, in the "empty" spaces in between. Consider the following verses from the Tao Te Ching commending the significance of mirroring, stillness, and emptiness:

Tao Te Ching, Verse 3 (excerpts)

The Master leads
by emptying people's minds
and filling their cores,
by weakening their ambition
and toughening their resolve.
He helps people lose everything
they know, everything they desire,
and creates confusion
in those who think that they know.

Practice not-doing,
and everything will fall into place (Lao Tzu, 1995)

Tao Te Ching, Verse 4

The way is empty,
used, but not used up.
Deep, yes! ancestral
to the ten thousand things

Blunting edge,
loosing bond,
dimming light,
the way is the dust of the way.

Quiet,
yes, and likely to endure.
Whose child? born
before the gods. (Lao Tzu, 2009, p. 8)

Tao Te Ching, Verse 11

Thirty spokes meet
in the hub
Where the wheel isn't
is where it's useful

Hollowed out,
clay makes a pot.
Where the pot's not
is where it's useful.

Cut doors and windows
to make a room.
Where the room isn't,
there's room for you.

So the profit in what is
is in the use of what isn't. (Lao Tzu, 2009, p. 17)

Tao Te Ching, Verse 15

The ancient Masters were profound and subtle.
Their wisdom was unfathomable.
There is no way to describe it;
all we can describe is their appearance.

They were careful
as someone crossing an iced-over stream.
Alert as a warrior in enemy territory.
Courteous as a guest.
Fluid as melting ice.
Shapable as a block of wood.
Receptive as a valley.
Clear as a glass of water.

Do you have the patience to wait
till your mud settles and the water is clear?
Can you remain unmoving
till the right action arises by itself?

The Master doesn't seek fulfillment.
Not seeking, not expecting,
she is present, and can welcome all things. (Lao Tzu, 1995)

Tao Te Ching, Verse 22

That which is incomplete becomes complete.
The crooked becomes straight,
The empty becomes full,
The worn-out becomes new.
He who obtains has little,
He who scatters has much.
That is why the self-controlled man holds to Unity and brings it into manifestation for men.
He looks not at self, therefore he sees clearly;
He asserts not himself, therefore he shines;
He boasts not of self, therefore he has merit;
He glorifies not himself, therefore he endures.
The Master indeed does not strive, yet no one in the world can strive against him.
The words of the Ancients were not empty words: "
That which is incomplete becomes complete."
Acquire completeness by returning it. (Lao Tzu, 2012, Chapter 6, para. 22)

Tao Te Ching, Verse 48 (excerpts)

To become learned, gain daily
To obtain Tao, reduce daily
Reduce and reduce again
    until all action is reduced to non-action
Then no one is left
Nothing is done
    yet nothing is left undone (Lao Tzu, 2003, p. 61)

The concept of emptying oneself is an important practice for many spiritual traditions. Johanson and Kurtz (1991) in their book titled *Grace Unfolding: Psychotherapy in the Spirit of the Tao Te Ching* pointed that the German theologian, philosopher, and mystic Meister Eckhardt taught that we find God through a process of subtraction rather than addition. They also referred to an ancient Jewish myth, which says that in the beginning, God was everything, so the only way God could create was by withdrawing, disappearing, to allow the space for life to emerge (Introduction, para 2). Similarly, Alan Watts (1957) points out:

> Indian philosophy concentrates on negation, on liberating the mind from concepts of Truth. It proposes no idea, no description, of what is to fill the mind's void because the idea would exclude the fact—somewhat as a picture of the sun on the windowpane would shut out the true sun's light. Whereas the Hebrews would not permit an image of God in wood or stone, the Hindus will not permit an image of thought—unless it be so obviously mythological as not to be mistaken for the reality. (Chapter 2, para. 32)

In the West, we are used to the accumulation of knowledge, and this is the common conception of supervision and the process of learning. However, the Taoist sages, along with numerous sages in other spiritual traditions, remind us of the importance of emptiness and letting go. This has important parallels when it comes to clinical training and the development of an existential therapist.

Given the significant utility of emptiness, it reinforces the importance for us to get out of the way of our supervisees' growth and teach them to get out of their own way and the way of their clients' growth. It is critical that we teach them the value of emptiness and how to create the necessary Khora space for their clients to grow into. This involves the emptying of ourselves, the letting go of our misplaced desires to be the helpful agent of change. This is what is meant by non-action. How, paradoxically, when nothing is done, when we have sufficiently reduced ourselves, nothing is left undone.

What is the process of emptiness? How do we go about emptying ourselves? In this regard, Zhuangzi (1998) offers the following three parables about nothingness, emptiness, and fasting of the mind:

> The Yellow Emperor was wandering north of Redwater when he ascended the heights of K'unlun and gazed toward the south. As he was returning home, he lost his pearl of mystery. Knowledge was sent to search for the pearl, but he couldn't find it. Spidersight was sent to search for the pearl, but he couldn't find it. Trenchancy (forceful, effective and vigorous) was sent to search for the pearl, but he couldn't find it, whereupon Amorphous was sent and he found it. "Extraordinary!" said the

> Yellow Emperor, "In the end, it was Amorphous who was able to find it." (p. 105)
>
> Woodworker Ch'ing was carving wood for a bellstand. When the bellstand was completed, all who saw it were amazed as though they were seeing the work of a spiritual being. The Marquis of Lu went to see it and inquired of the woodworker, saying, "With what art have you made this?"
>
> "Your subject is merely a workman," was the reply. "What art could I possess? However, there is one thing. When I am getting ready to make a bellstand, I dare not waste any of my energy, so it is necessary to fast in order to calm my mind. After fasting for three days, I no longer presume to harbor any thoughts of congratulations and rewards, of rank and salary. After fasting for five days, I no longer presume to harbor any thoughts of censure or praise, of skill or clumsiness. After fasting for seven days, I abruptly forget that I have four limbs and a body. At that time, I have no thoughts of public affairs or the court. My skill is concentrated and all external distractions disappear. Only then do I enter the mountain forest and observe the heavenly nature of the trees till I find one of ultimate form. Only after the completed bellstand manifests itself to me do I set my hands to the work. Otherwise, I give up. Thus is heaven joined to heaven. This is what makes one suspect that my instruments were made by a spiritual being." (p. 183)
>
> "Maintaining the unity of your will," said Confucius, "listen not with your ears but with your mind. Listen not with your mind but with your primal breath. The ears are limited to listening, the mind is limited to tallying. The primal breath, however, awaits things emptily. It is only through the Way that one can gather emptiness, and emptiness is the fasting of the mind." (p.32)

As to letting go, I tell my supervisees that when a neophyte psychotherapist sits in the room with their client for the first time, there are two people struggling with anxiety—and that I'm sure their anxiety will be much greater than that of the client. So if you can simply survive those first sessions and manage to deal sufficiently with your own anxiety, then your first sessions can be considered a success. Develop a closer relationship with your own anxiety before considering being helpful with your clients' anxiety. If possible, let go of your desire to heal your client, and hopefully, your client will return for the second session. The sad truth, of course, is, that often they don't return, which is the painful truth of clinical training.

Companionship and Existential Isolation

My first client did not return after the first session. It was very difficult for me to accept. She was a large black woman whose presenting issue I have now long forgotten. And I was an introverted Asian male. Our two cultures could not have been further apart. I was unsuccessful in bridging our worlds, not to mention empathically entering into hers. My world, my short lived-experience during that session was pure chaos, desperately trying to find solutions to her problems and thus alleviate my anxiety and repair some semblance of my young ego. No wonder my client chose not to return. I would not have. I recall walking around campus for an hour after my initial session, discouraged and angry with the people who ran my clinical training program. I thought to myself, how can they abandon me to be all alone in that therapy room? Why was there not more support? Why did I have to be paired with someone so entirely different from me as my first client? Why me? My anger and discouragement were such that I thought about quitting the program. I finally decided against doing so because my hefty tuition for the year was already paid and I did not want to be a quitter. My pride and ego took a huge hit. Yet ironically, it was also my pride that kept me from calling it quits.

There was not a lot I could do to nurture my wounded and fragile ego back then. I don't remember how much help or nurturance I received from my first supervisor. It was too long ago. All I do remember is that it is a scar, and now I realize that it is a necessary scar, one among many that are an important part of becoming a seasoned psychotherapist and a compassionate supervisor. Even though I now realize that the scar of surviving that first session is part of the painful path of becoming a competent psychotherapist, the pain of that scar is occasionally brought back when I help guide my supervisees through their own chaotic and anxiety-filled first sessions. The pain is also revisited when my current clients do not return, leaving me to question my abilities. I realize that the pain I experienced is the essence of my patience and compassion now. Perhaps I was "destined" to experience that painful rejection so that I can now be a source of compassion for the suffering of my supervisees. At the very least, it is the meaning that I now ascribe to my scar that makes it the beautiful part of my existence.

For in the beautiful words crafted by the Austrian poet Rainer Maria Rilke (n.d.):

> Do not assume that he who seeks to comfort you now, lives untroubled among the simple and quiet words that sometimes do you good. His life may also have much sadness and difficulty, that remains far beyond yours. Were it otherwise, he would never have been able to find these words.

Rollo May (1981) also taught me that "The past cannot be changed —it can only be acknowledged and learned from. It is one's destiny. It can be absorbed and mitigated by new experiences, but it cannot be changed or erased . . . If we can accept our destiny, the fates will work *with* rather than *against* us. In this way, we live with the universe rather than against it" (pp. 35–37). And Victor Frankl (1985) taught me that questions of "why me" ultimately bring very little relief when it comes to suffering. Instead, he teaches:

> What was really needed was a fundamental change in our attitude towards life. We had to learn ourselves and, furthermore, we had to teach the despairing men that it does not really matter what we expect from life, but rather what life expects from us. We needed to stop asking about the meaning of life, and instead to think of ourselves as those who were being questioned by life—daily and hourly. Our answer must consist not in talk and meditation, but in right action and in right conduct. Life ultimately means taking the responsibility to find the right answers to its problems and to fulfill the tasks which it constantly sets for each individual. (p. 98)

The fact that clients are sometimes sacrificed is the untold truth of clinical training, and it is not limited to the field of psychotherapy. One of my favorite American TV shows was ER (Emergency Room), which aired from 1994 to 2009. One particular scene and quote have always stayed with me. The made-for-TV drama incident was one in which a new doctor was struggling and punishing himself for overlooking a physical symptom that led to the death of his patient. It was at this moment that the hard-nose attending physician in the ER told him that "you don't become a good doctor until you've killed your first patient!" What a cruel but truthful and perhaps comforting thing to say. In fact, I'm glad that I'm knocked out with anesthesia during an operation at a teaching hospital. I'd hate to be privy to the conversation between the head surgeon and the surgeon in training. Yet, they have it better than we psychologists in some ways. At least someone is looking over their shoulders supervising their work. Our first sessions with our clients are deep experiences of existential isolation. There is no one to look over our shoulders and whisper in our ears. No one can tell us how to conduct our sessions. We must walk that path alone. Psychotherapy is an inherently lonely endeavor. If clients only knew of the loneliness that we therapists must also endure, the same loneliness and isolation that our clients are themselves struggling with. And if they were privy to the machinations of our mind, our clients and supervisees would see that the companionship goes both ways. That at the center of a deep encounter are two isolated individuals coming together to provide companionship on each other's lonely existential journeys.

Isolation and Anxiety

Along with isolation, there is also anxiety. It is not only the beginning psychotherapist who must manage anxiety. From an existential perspective, anxiety is an inescapable part of being a free man. As long as you're alive, you will experience anxiety. It's just that as we progress and develop as individuals and clinicians, we are better able to manage our anxiety. It is never the absence of anxiety. If significant healing or growth is to take place, therapists must journey into dark, hidden places of the client's lives and into the emptiness of existence itself. And our ability to tolerate and manage that anxiety, the anxiety of helplessness, the anxiety of being lost, even the anxiety of hopelessness must be endured if we are to be a healing presence for our clients.

The ability to sit with our anxiety is reflected in the following parable from Zhuangzi (2013):

> Once there was a man who was afraid of his shadow and who hated his footprints, and so he tried to get away from them by running. But the more he lifted his feet and put them down again, the more footprints he made. And no matter how fast he ran, his shadow never left him, and so, thinking that he was still going too slowly, he ran faster and faster without a stop until his strength gave out and he fell down dead. He didn't understand that by lolling in the shade he could have gotten rid of his shadow and that by resting in quietude he could have put

> an end to his footprints. How could he have been so stupid! (Chapter 31, para. 22)

Self-Compassion

Yet I digress. Let me return to that beginning therapist that we all once were, and some of you are now. The unspoken brutal reality is that oftentimes clients are sacrificed in the course of training. This is unavoidable. I'm sure many of us can think back to all of the ways we could have served our clients better. I know that all of us have agonized over clients who have not returned. So one of the messages that I'm constantly preaching from pulpits large and small is that if we are to survive and even thrive in this field of work, *we need to practice compassion with ourselves.* This is not true only in the field of psychotherapy but in the bright lights and on the hardcourts of the National Basketball Association (NBA) as well. Phil Jackson wrote that even though compassion was not a word bandied about much in the male-ego-dominated locker rooms of the NBA, self-compassion was one of the key building blocks in his work as a coach. He offered the following quote from Buddhist teacher Pema Chodron about how meditation practice blurs the traditional boundaries between self and others: "What you do for yourself—any gesture of kindness, any gesture of gentleness, any gesture of honesty and clear seeing toward yourself—will affect how you experience the world," she writes. "What you do for yourself, you're doing for others, and what you do for others, you're doing for yourself" (Jackson & Delehanty, 2013, Chapter 4, para. 60). One would not naturally associate self-compassion with winning basketball championships. Yet Phil Jackson understands that it is much easier to tear down an opponent than to build someone up. It is always easier to hurt rather than heal. Jackson has eleven championship rings, and many of his players swear by him. Surely there is something to the paradoxical wisdom of blending self-compassion with the warrior mentality that we can learn from.

So the best way to learn about how to be compassionate and empathic towards your clients is to first practice it on oneself. Yet, it is amazing to me how compassionate my supervisees can be towards their clients and at the same time be so brutally critical of their own work. I'm no different. So at the very least, as a supervisor, I often remind my students of our need for grace. Resilience is key to any accomplishment. Yet, resilience is not only this gritting-of-your teeth form of tenacity and endurance. It is also the soft yielding of grace and compassion. So I've told my supervisees that I fully expect them to lose clients in the midst of their training. For a few who are overly cautious and critical of themselves, I even give them special permission to lose clients. Yet paradoxically, it is when my students learn to let go, when I can let go of some of my expectations, that more of their clients end up staying with them. Why? The reasons are numerous and complex. Recall verse 38 of the Tao Te Ching discussed earlier in this chapter: When we master Wu Wei (non-action) nothing is undone. Part of it, I believe, has to do with their being. It has something to do with the way they were with themselves and with their clients. They've let go of their own expectations and learned to sit with their anxiety and in the process were more able to tune into and sit with their clients' anxiety. They stopped running away from their shadows. They've learned something about the power of grace. They learned about faith. They practiced self-compassion and were thus more empathic and compassionate toward their clients. They've learned to understand Roger's paradoxical statement that "acceptance is the beginning of change."

Perfection

Like the supervisees discussed above, we all tend to feel overly responsible for the growth of our clients, especially when we are feeling particularly inadequate ourselves. This over-assumption of responsibility is also about the pursuit of perfection and its converse, the fear of failure. Emily Han is a graduate student I met at one of my workshops in Malaysia. She is also learning about the ways of the Tao and naturally developed a strong interest in existential psychology. Emily taught me that perfection is not about the upward, vertical pursuit of being the best of the best. Instead, from a Taoist perspective, it is about achieving a perfect balance that I visualize more along a horizontal plane. This parallels the concept of horizontalization within phenomenological psychology. I agree with Emily that this form of balance is a more inclusive form of beauty and much more difficult to achieve. Beauty involves symmetry, and symmetry is about balance. It does not exclude or privilege one over the other. Moreover, trying to be the best is an extreme, and the pursuit of the extreme causes one to lose balance and subsequently fall or fail. In thinking about balance, I visualize the Cicada Catcher in Zhuangzi's parable listed earlier in this chapter, being limberly erect, balancing his pallets at the end of his stick. Similarly, note the symbolism of the erect but withered stinktree with twisted roots. Far from perfection wouldn't you say?

If perfection is about achieving balance, then balance involves both success and failure. I recall a supervisor during my graduate training remarking that seasoned clinicians are likely to be helpful to one-third of their clientele, somewhat helpful to another third, and not much help at all to the remaining third. I remember thinking at that time that these were terrible odds and could not possibly be true. Which healthcare profession would readily accept such odds? Surely this must be an exaggeration! We may debate the finer points of this observation through questions such as: Can we consider this last one-third of our caseload to be true "failures?" I suppose it's a matter of perspective. Or are these ratios too simplistic and out of balance? Surely, as we gain experience, we will begin to alter the ratio toward additional successes. What cannot be denied however is that failure is inseparable from success, as described by the following verses from the Tao Te Ching. We cannot truly appreciate our successes without experiencing failure. Indeed our failures are the seeds to our success. For life is about refinement and not perfection. The best that we can hope for, as we become more aware of our weaknesses, is that we will make fewer of our usual mistakes. Perfection, the absence of mistakes is a dangerous illusion. Heaven forbid what will become of our egos without the counterbalancing limitations of failure. And what better time to begin learning about failure, self-compassion, and forgiveness than right at the inception of our training? Thus, supervisors play a critical role in this regard. It is through our compassion and unconditional positive regard for our supervisees that they learn about self-compassion and forgiveness and thus pass this experience onto their clients. And in all honesty, learning self-compassion and forgiveness is an ongoing lesson. Failure to help our clients is part of the natural balance of conducting therapy, and the better we're able to embrace failure and recognize this balance, the closer we will come to achieving perfection. In the words of the Tao Te Ching:

Tao Te Ching, Verse 13 (excerpts)

"Be wary of both honor and disgrace"
"Endless affliction is bound to the body"

What does it mean,
  "Be wary of both honor and disgrace"?
Honor is founded on disgrace
  and disgrace is rooted in honor.

Both should be avoided
Both bind a man to this world
That's why it says,
"Be wary of both honor and disgrace" (Lao Tzu, 2003, p. 26)

Tao Te Ching, Verse 44 (excerpts)

Fame or integrity: which is more important?
Money or happiness: which is more valuable?
Success or failure: which is more destructive? (Lao Tzu, 1995)

The Perfect Book Store

Finally, Margaret and the vision/illusion of her Perfect Bookstore serves as an excellent illustration of this Taoist concept of perfection. Margaret is a book worm who has long dreamed of opening a bookstore and sharing her passion for books with others. She is a therapist, a visionary, and inspired student of existential psychology in China. Margaret is very unconventional in the sense that she approaches the finances of the bookstore with a gambling-entertainment mindset. She is realistic about the financial investment necessary for operating a bookstore. She informed me that she's set aside a certain amount of money for the operation of the bookstore. She's not sure how long this amount of money will last but she's prepared for the bookstore to remain open as long as this money is available. This reminds me of those who go to casinos knowing fully that they are more than likely to lose. Yet, they understand that the amount they've set aside is considered "entertainment expenses." So to them, it's not a losing proposition. Instead, it's an investment in an experience. Margaret holds the same perspective. She understands that she's investing in an experience without knowing how long this experience will last. She works hard to operate the bookstore knowing that she will be moving on to another life experience when the money runs out.

Like Ving, Margaret is quite atypical (or perhaps not so atypical for those who dare to pursue their dream of opening a coffee shop or small café/bookstore). Part of Margaret's dream for this bookstore is the creation of a space/place where people can come to reflect and get back in touch with their souls. She desires for the place to be inviting and safe. A place of trust and nurturance. A Khora space. I've participated in and supported Margaret's bookstore dream by holding several small seminars focused on existential psychology. I've experienced the intimacy and warmth of the space.

Thus, it was painful for me to receive a call from Margaret one morning to learn that she found about a half month's wages missing in cash from her purse. The theft took place during an informal lunch gathering in her bookstore. She had a very good idea who stole the money from her because the thief must be familiar with where she stores her cash. Margaret had known the thief as a trusted friend who previously received several loans from Margaret during her time of need. And upon further revelation, Margaret shared that this was not the first time such thievery has taken place. Margaret admitted to dismissing the likelihood of betrayal before. Surely such betrayal could not happen in paradise (her perfect bookstore). Perhaps the money was simply "borrowed" on previous occasions. But this time, there is no denying that money indeed has been stolen. Paradise became tainted and imperfect as other friends shared with her that such thievery was indeed commonplace.

Margaret poured her heart out and shared with me the pain and meaning of her loss. I empathized with the pain of betrayal and the loss of innocence. Margaret worked hard to create a small piece of paradise in a dark world but darkness crept into her place of light. More painful than the financial loss was the loss of innocence and the loss of a dream. She can no longer roam freely in paradise and be carefree about security. She will now have to be on guard in her own "home." She dreaded having to grow up to this reality.

Yet, as Margaret shared her story and begin to make meaning out of it, the lessons of our trainings in existential psychology began to take hold for her. She thought about the reality of evil. She reacquainted herself with imperfection. She reflected deeper upon paradox. I shared with her about how I'm learning from my colleague Jason Dias about balancing rather than resolving paradoxes. Jason taught me that "paradoxes do not require a solution. The solution to a paradox is to grow large enough to contain the various meanings suggested by the problem, to stop insisting that only one thing be true at one time" (Yang, 2017, p. 31)

Rollo May (1969) wrote in *Love and Will*:

> The only way to resolving – contrast to solving – the questions is to transform them by means of deeper and wider dimensions of consciousness. The problems must be embraced in their full meaning, the antinomies (a contradiction between two

> statements, both apparently obtained by correct reasoning) resolved even with their contradictions. They must be built upon; and out of this will arise a new level of consciousness. This is as close as we shall ever get to a resolution; and it is all we need to get. In psychotherapy, for example, we do not seek answers as such, or cut and dry solutions to the question – which would leave the patient worse off than he originally was in his struggling. But we seek to help him take in, encompass, embrace, and integrate the problem. With insight, Carl Jung once remarked that the serious problems of life are never solved, and if it seems that they have been solved, something important has been lost. (pp. 307–308)

Following the same theme, elsewhere May (1994) also wrote that "insights emerge not chiefly because they are 'rationally true' or even helpful, but because they have a certain form, the form that is beautiful because it completes an incomplete Gestalt" (p. 68).

Finally, Margaret shared with me that it was time for her to face the reality of evil. To face the pain she ran away from before. Margaret is learning about how darkness and light are co-constituted and how perfection encompasses the imperfect. Margaret shared that she's glad that her perfect bookstore is now mature enough to include the imperfect. I shared with Margaret that she paid the tuition for both of us. That through her lesson, I'm becoming just a bit larger to contain the imperfect within my being as well. I look forward to my next visit to the Perfect Bookstore.

The Decrepit Bar

After introducing the Perfect Bookstore, it is only proper that I also make your acquaintance with Fannings and the Decrepit Bar, which is located near the vicinity of the Perfect Bookstore. I was introduced to Fannings by Margaret when I returned to her bookstore to give a workshop on the topic of the interdependence between life and death. When I visited the actual bar, I found that bar was not dilapidated but quite unique for it functioned as a gelato stand, pet hospice, charitable temple, secular confessional, jazz performance center (a venue for numerous impromptu jam sessions), and hug factory. Fannings, the young owner affectionately referred to her bar as decrepit when in fact it was quaint and filled with the spirit of classical Suzhou (near Shanghai China). The actual name of the bar was Locke Bar named after the English philosopher John Locke, the Father of Classical Liberalism. Fannings herself embodied such a spirit of liberation, the same wandering spirit that Zhuangzi (1998) wrote about in the first chapter of his book titled *Carefree Wandering*.

Fannings was a psychology major in college. She worked at a counseling center for a while after graduation but decided to leave that job and open a bar because she felt like she could best actualize herself and serve others by creating a place of happiness as opposed to misery. Though soon, Fannings realized that happiness and misery and pain and joy are intertwined. Fannings would summarize her learning thusly: "Story after story, everyone's the same." Through listening to countless stories, she discovered the well-known "secret" that bars are secular confessionals. I shared with her Irvin Yalom's writing where he highlighted the wisdom of French writer Andre Malraux, who once asked a parish priest who had been hearing confessions for 50 years what he had learned about mankind. The priest replied, "First of all, people are much more unhappy than one thinks . . . and then the fundamental fact is that there is no such thing as a grown-up person" (Yalom, 1980, p. 13). Fannings agreed wholeheartedly and added, "Yeah, all these corporate types are just average Joes all dressed up." In the end, Fannings and I joked that the Locke Bar was perhaps the only democratic bar in communist China!

Part of the dream behind the bar was Fannings' desire to create a space for people to gather and express themselves. This is accomplished through regularly organized and impromptu jam sessions that take place at her bar. Additional opportunities for creative outlets include poetry readings and music events such as Arabian Nights! Her patrons reciprocate her hospitality and munificence through gifts of books and musical instruments, thus expanding her bar by making it part of their home away from home. Fanning proudly shared that the bar's foreign library and musical stage came into being spontaneously without any financial outlay on her part. Indeed many of her patrons are foreigners who hunger for a "place where everyone knows your name." This was validated by writers from The Lonely Planet travel guide book series, who included the Locke Bar as one of the recommended sites to visit in Suzhou.

Of course, the pursuit and realization of Fanning's dreams is not without its price. All business owners know, cash flow is a constant struggle, especially when one of your partners runs off with all of your cash reserves! But as was discussed in the workshop at the Perfect Bookstore, "stars shine brightest during the darkest of nights" (Persian proverb). And it is during periods of vulnerability and need when we discover the truth behind Paulo Coehlo's (2006) proclamation that "No heart has ever suffered when it goes in search of its dream" (p. 283) and that "When you want something, all the universe conspires in helping you to achieve it" (p. 60).[1] Finding herself without money to pay the rent for her own abode and the bar, Fanning asked for help through Facebook. The support was overwhelming. Fanning's original request was for housing for one week. A bar patron and friend responded by offering to share her apartment for six months. In addition, Fanning found the fridge consistently well stocked upon her return from work in the early mornings. Other patrons offered unconditional loans for the bar's monthly rent, which Fannings was able to repay within eight months through the numerous free mini-concerts that were held there. Business was booming because people were more than enthusiastic to repay Fanning's original kindness and hospitality.

After such experiences of largess, no wonder Fannings related that the Decrepit Bar also occasionally functioned as a temple. As I was talking with Fannings late into the night in the back of the bar, I was surprised that Fannings left her small gelato stand at the front of the store unattended. Don't you worry about thieves, Fannings? Are you crazy? Fannings was unfazed and considered the question complimentary for Fannings understood herself as a "weirdo" viewed through the eyes of conventional society. Fannings shared that thievery was uncommon but when it occurs, the thief must have been in need! Huh! I was dumbstruck! Fannings went on to describe how temples in Japan would regularly put out money, food, and clothing in an unlocked box for people in need. This was the first time that I'd heard of a bar functioning as a temple. Weird indeed!

What is not weird is the fact that the bar also functions as a pet hospice: People will leave their dying pets at the bar's doorsteps knowing that the owner of the Decrepit Bar will choose to provide their pets the necessary painful but rewarding companionship through the last chapter of their brief lives. Why and how does Fannings accomplish this? I suspect that without verbalizing the following teachings by Buddhist teacher Pema Chodron, Fannings knew that

> only to the extent that we expose ourselves over and over to annihilation can that which is indestructible be found in us.

---

[1] These same circumstances and quotes by Paulo Coehlo can also be found in the story of Ving and her coffee shop, spread throughout the various chapters in this book.

> Things falling apart is a kind of testing and also a kind of healing. We think that the point is to pass the test or to overcome the problem, but the truth is that things don't really get solved. They come together again and fall apart again. It's just like that. The healing comes from letting there be room for all of this to happen: room for grief, for relief, for misery, for joy (Chodron 1997, pp. 9–10).

Indeed Fannings shared that each time she cries over the death of a cat she's had to euthanize the pain is just as intense. It does not hurt any less. However, she says, "I also find that I'm also much more able to move on and recover from that loss." Just like the physical space that she has created in the interior of the Decrepit Bar, Fannings has created within herself the inner space for grief, relief, misery, and joy.

Upon hearing about Fanning's stories of her pet hospice, I shared the following two stories with Fanning. I told her about the play *Let Me Down Easy,* by Anna Deavere Smith. In this play, one of the characters portrayed was a remarkable woman who cared for African children with AIDS. Little help was available at her shelter. Children died every day. When asked what she did to ease the dying children's terror, she answered with two phrases: "I never let them die alone in the dark, and I say to them, 'You will always be with me here in my heart'" (Yalom, 2008, p. 132).

Similarly, Kent Brantly, an American doctor and graduate of Indiana University School of Medicine (2015) gave the following talk at a college graduation ceremony in May of 2015:

> In the first seven weeks of treating patients with Ebola, we had only one survivor; one survivor and nearly 20 deaths. Losing so many patients certainly was difficult. But it didn't make me feel like a failure as a physician, because I had learned that there's a lot more to being a physician than curing illness. In fact, that isn't even the most important thing we do. The most important thing we do is to enter into the suffering of others. And in the midst of what was becoming the worst Ebola epidemic in history, we were showing compassion to people during the most desperate and trying times of their lives. Through the protection of Tyvek suits and two pairs of gloves, we were able to hold the hands of people as they died to offer dignity in the face of humiliating circumstances, to treat with respect the

> dying and the dead. And in my opinion, that made those weeks, those difficult weeks of my career a success.

I know that for Fannings, the companionship she provides for her dying pets is an essential part of the success of the Decrepit Bar.

Finally, Fannings shared her most treasured reward for opening the Decrepit Bar. During the workshop, numerous students shared how much they desired physical affection from their parents and how difficult it was for them to ask for and for the parents to give out something as simple as a hug. This lack of affection in China is ubiquitous. The pain in the room for Fannings was as palpable as the missing hugs themselves. Yet it was at this point that Fannings smiled her biggest smile. She shared that she, too, wanted but could not ask her mother for a hug that the mother was very unaccustomed to give. Indeed, one of the workshop participants shared that when she first initiated a hug with her mother, her mother wondered aloud if her daughter was emotionally disturbed! Fannings went on to share that her mother was initially very unsupportive of her bar. Her mother's first comment upon her initial tour of the bar was to ask Fannings when she would be through with her hobby and ready to get on with a real job! However, after two weeks of feeling for herself the hospitality, generosity, misery, pain, connectedness, and physical affection displayed in the bar, the mother spontaneously gave Fannings her blessing through a hug upon her departure. It was just part of the territory, a natural occurrence in the Decrepit Bar. Fannings shared that one spontaneous and unsolicited hug from her mother was rationale enough and justified the existence of her Decrepit Bar. Who are we argue otherwise!

Fannings description of her Decrepit Bar brings to mind Zhuangzi's parable of the Useless Tree, which appeared in Chapter 2. Fanning's affinity for the decrepit, discarded, vulnerable, weird, and uncommon would make any Taoists proud. Like the Useless Tree described below in Zhuangzi's parable. Fannings understood that the beauty and secret to the survival of the Useless Tree lay in its uselessness.[2] Like the useless tree, the dying pets that others drop off on her doorstep are broken, gnarled, and knotted. Sadly, in the eyes of their owners, they are beyond their usefulness. Having met Mina, one of her dog rescues, I

---

[2] Readers who are interested in a more in-depth analysis of this parable can refer to Chapter One of *Existential Psychology and the Way of the Tao: Meditations on the Writings of Zhuangzi* published by Routledge, 2017.

can testify that the parallels to the symbol of the stinktree are more than symbolic, for Mina's breath and body odor were something only Fannings could love. It is understandable why Mina would be "heeded by no one." Nevertheless, Fannings showered heaps of love on Mina and cried her eyes out when she had to be euthanized. True to the spirit of Zhuangzi's parable, like Dr. Brantly above, Fannings was willing to enter into Mina's suffering and the suffering of numerous others, just like the useless tree stinktree that survives to provide refuge and shelter amid the wastelands. What a beautiful Decrepit Bar, next to the Perfect Bookstore in the middle of Suzhou, China.

Preparation

Nevertheless, my students, especially the responsible students, will ask me how they can serve their clients if they do not prepare adequately ahead of time. I always offer them the same paradoxical answer. As you can tell, we existentialists have this thing for paradox. I tell my students that I have both good news and bad news. First of all, the bad news. I tell them that they can never be adequately prepared for their sessions. I am not advising my students not to prepare or read materials in order to be better educated about their clients. Indeed, they must not abandon their readings and training for the accumulation of knowledge and experience is an important part of becoming a better therapist. However, paradoxically, they must also not forget to leave their readings, their techniques, their prepared plans at the door upon entering the room. For how else how are they going to be attuned to the client sitting in front of them at the time versus the imaginary client they prepared for? Which client are you going to meet and care for? So I tell my supervisees that they can never truly be "prepared" for their sessions for you don't know what your clients will bring to you. Thus, prioritize presence over preparedness. This is the bad news. See what I mean about anxiety!

Then comes the good news!

The good news is that you have been preparing all your life for these sessions. At this point, I usually get a funny look from my supervisees. I then ask them, "How much of what you've learned in class and from your books, do you apply and use when you meet with your clients?" If they are honest, they will admit that very little of what they actually use and say to their clients come from the lectures or the books. Then I ask them, "How much of what you share with your clients comes out of your own lived experiences, including the novels you've read recently and the movie that you watched last week, the song that won't leave your head, the innumerable joy and pain that you've paid for with blood?" At this point, they understand what I'm driving at. My supervisees like it quite a bit when I tell them never to forgo their interests and hobbies. Graduate schools in the United States can be a long grind. Many give up their hobbies, pastimes, and even their important relationships in the pursuit of that degree. We teach holistic living, but we don't allow our supervisees to live holistically. We talk about being centered and balanced, yet we fill their brains at the expense of their hearts. The ironic and tragic danger of learning psychology is that one can easily lose one's humanity. Our clients become cases. We treat cases rather than people. We refer to their diagnosis rather than their names. We treat them as objects to be manipulated and "treated" rather than human beings that require our love and attention. So, once again, it's about letting go and letting it be. Ontology. Following the way of the Tao. Nature is not in a hurry, and yet everything gets done. Such a way of being is difficult to teach and learn in a direct manner. Nevertheless, it can be cultivated and nurtured. The thing is, we've been learning all our lives to be the therapists we are. And it will take the rest of our lives to become the therapists we want to be.

The Courage of the Therapist

As discussed earlier, one of the hallmarks of a good therapist is the ability to sit with anxiety. Anxiety is a fancier word for fear. What is it that overcomes fear but courage? My colleague Francis Kaklauskas shared with me something that his supervisor shared with him once. His supervisor told him that what earns us the right to be someone's therapist is not our credentials but our courage—our courage to journey with our clients into dark places of despair, places of helplessness, hopelessness, and emptiness. Zhuangzi (2013) described such courage thusly:

> "To travel across the water without shrinking from the sea serpent or the dragon—this is the courage of the fisherman. To travel over land without shrinking from the rhinoceros or the tiger—this is the courage of the hunter. To see the bare blades clashing before him and to look on death as though it were life—this is the courage of the man of ardor. To understand that hardship is a matter of fate, that success is a matter of the times,

and to face great difficulty without fear—this is the courage of the sage. (Chapter 17, para. 36)

Lieh Yukou was demonstrating his archery for Uncle Obscure Nobody. He drew the bow to its full extent, had someone place a cup of water on his elbows, and release the string. No sooner had he shot the first arrow than he nocked another, and as soon as he shot the second arrow another was lodged on the nocking point. All the while he stood like a statue.

Uncle Obscure Nobody said, "This is the archery of an archer, not the archery of a nonarcher. Let's climb a high mountain and clamber over steep rocks until we overlook a chasm one hundred fathoms deep. Will you be able to shoot then?"

Thereupon Nobody and Yukou climbed a high mountain and clambered over steep rocks until they were overlooking a chasm one hundred fathoms deep. Nobody inched out backward so that his feet were halfway over the edge. He bowed to Yukou and invited him to come forward, but Yukou had fallen prostrate on the ground, with sweat dripping down to his heels.

"The ultimate man," said Uncle Obscure Nobody, "peers into the cerulean sky above and descends into the Yellow Springs below. Though he roams to the eight ends of the universe, his spirit and vitality undergo no transformation. But now the timorousness of your will shows in your dazed eyes. Your inner state of being is in peril."

Confucius heard of this and said, "The true man of old could not be persuaded by those who are cunning, could not be seduced by beautiful women, could not be plundered by robbers, could not be befriended by Fushi and the Yellow Emperor. Life and death are of great moment, but they could effect no transformation upon him, how much less rank and salary? This being so, his spirit might pass over a great mountain without impediment, enter a deep spring without getting wet, dwell in humble circumstances without feeling wretched. He was filled with heaven and earth, so that the more he gave to others, the more he had for himself." (Zhuangzi, 1998, pp. 206–208, excerpts)

When it comes down to it, what is most important is the courage to stay present and face the fear. Here, a hospice social worker describes what it's like to help a grieving family:

> Maybe the most important thing I can offer is the willingness to sit beside them without flinching as thoughts and feelings, however intense, tumble out. I can bear witness. I can trust that, however desperate things seem on the surface, underneath, each second is full of meaning and possibility." My mind drifts to a conversation I had years ago with a clinical supervisor who said, "Ninety percent of this work is having the guts to show up and look at what's happening without changing the subject." (Janssen, n.d.).

Why journey into the darkness? Why such dismal focus on anxiety and pain? A famous reporter once asked a convicted bank robber why he robbed banks. The robber replied nonchalantly, "That is where the money is." So why plunge into the abyss with our clients? "Because if a way to the best be found, it exacts a full look at the worst" (Hardy, n.d.). Nietzsche (n.d.[b]) said, "to become wise, you must learn to listen to the wild dogs barking in your cellar." Terence (n.d.), a second-century Roman playwright, offers an aphorism that is extraordinarily important in the inner work of the therapist: "I am human, and I consider nothing that is human alien to me." No matter how brutal, cruel, forbidden, or alien a client's experience, can you locate in yourself some affinity to it? Are you willing to enter into your own darkness for Lao Tzu (1995) reminded us in the last sentence of verse one, the most well-known verse of the *Tao Te Ching*:

> Yet mystery and manifestations
> Arise from the same source.
> The source is darkness
>
> Darkness within darkness.
> The gateway to all understanding.

This point was brought home to me by a friend here in China recently. She confronted me regarding my notion of myself being a good man. This is a long-cherished notion that I have of myself. It is an image that I labor to keep. Yet, she confronted me about how I can call myself an existential psychologist if I do not see and own up to my own evil.

Not only my pain and despair but my own evil. I desperately do not want to see this part of myself. Even less so do I want to show this part to others. I loathe this part! However, if I am to take Terence's words seriously, that "I am human and I consider nothing that is human alien to me," then I must take seriously my own evil nature. This is a work in progress—a work that will require more grace than I have for myself at this point. Currently, I am learning the grace to be patient with myself. Be gentle with yourself, Mark. Be gentle.

Lilac

Finally, I'd like to offer you a supervision case that I was privileged to be a part of. It comes courtesy of an extraordinary individual named Bruce. Bruce is now a mentor himself, teaching about existential–humanistic psychology throughout Hong Kong and China. Bruce shared with me a beautiful encounter he had with a patient he was asked to help at the palliative ward of a hospital in southern China. The patient was an elderly gentleman who was suffering from pain related to his terminal-stage stomach cancer. The inoperable cancer had metastasized to his intestines, lungs, and other internal organs. He completed eight rounds of chemotherapy in an attempt to arrest the metastasis. Yet the pain intensified after every treatment, leaving the patient in a constant foul mood. Upon entry into the six-bed hospital room, Bruce found a man who was gaunt, with an extended belly. He appeared older than his chronological age and presented a very tough appearance. The room was crowded with other patients and family members. A number of the other patients had their radios on. The room was anything but tranquil.

The patient was a communist official who was having difficulty accepting the terminal stage of his cancer. The doctors informed the patient that he had only six to twelve months to live. Yet, the patient refused to believe this news and instead adopted an optimistic and rosy attitude that he could overcome cancer in the same way he had overcome numerous obstacles in his life as a soldier. Bruce was wise and decided not to challenge the patient's entrenched hope and beliefs.

Instead, Bruce shared with the patient the story of another cancer patient whose unfinished business was to witness the first day of school for his grandson. The patient immediately related to the story and shared with Bruce that his son was recently married and planned to have a child the following year. The patient's wish was to live to see the birth of his grandchild before his death. This tough soldier broke down in tears while describing the image of holding, feeding, and playing with his grandson. It was in the midst of such reverie when the patient in a hushed tone suddenly revealed a second, more intimate dying wish.

As it turns out, the patient had married his pre-arranged wife under the pressure of family and tradition. The marriage was long and stable but without love. The patient described the wife as responsible but he did not love her. Instead, his heart remained with his first love, who had died of a terminal illness. This first love was his true love, and together they had rebelled against the wishes of their families and society. It was likely that they would have married each other if not for her premature death. And ever since the death of his lover, he visited her grave frequently, often bringing along a bundle of lilacs, her favorite flower. Unfortunately, the patient ended the visits to the grave when he became immobile as the result of his illness. So the patient's intimate dying wish was to visit his lover's grave one more time, bringing along her favorite flower, and sing to her their love song was, which also named Lilac.

However, the reality of the situation was that the man was immobile and unable to leave the hospital to complete this last wish. So the question I often ask my supervisees is, "What would you do at this point if you were Bruce? What is the proper 'intervention' here? What would you do if you knew or did not know this classic love song?"

Most students at this point talked about doing something for the patient. Ideas ranged from writing a letter to recording a videotape of the patient singing the song to bring to the grave of his first love. They reasoned that if the patient could not travel to the grave, why not bring the grave to the patient. There was no denying my students' desire to help. Everyone thought of solutions and what they can "do" to be of help to the patient.

Yet Bruce was no ordinary student and trainee. Upon hearing the name of the song, deep powerful images flooded Bruce's consciousness: bittersweet memories of his own hospital visits bearing flowers of his own; tears of joy, bitterness, and anger; forgotten promises made long ago. Bruce knew this song quite well. At a point of inspiration and deep identification, Bruce deepened the encounter by asking his client if he would like for Bruce to sing this song to/with him? The patient nodded. Mind you, this was taking place in a crowded public hospital room with other patients and family present and several radios blaring.

Nevertheless, Bruce went ahead and sang the song a cappella. After the first line of the song, the patient closed his eyes and began to cry. Following the melody, the patient sang along silently with Bruce. The offering of song shifted Bruce and the man to another world. Slowly, the room became quiet. The radios were respectfully silenced, and the other patients began to gather around the bed of this patient. The room of strangers converged and naturally formed an instant support group, at the center of which was this dying man. A spontaneous, impromptu universe was created where the other patients focused their good wishes and healing energy on this man, who was everyman. Time and pain were suspended, and everyone entered into *The Eternal Now* (title of one of Paul Tillich's [1963] books). The man was unable to travel to the grave. However, through the song, Bruce transported the man and the other patients and their families to a deep place of connection. He brought the man back to his lover for a final goodbye. The other individuals in the room quickly became participants in this here-and-now drama, themselves temporarily and eternally transported to individual hallowed places of tranquility and connection. A powerful dose of existential analgesic was administered. Time stood still, ironically, in the midst of singing a song about transience, detachment, impermanence, and death.

Such are the moments of transformation and healing. Bruce was wise beyond his years. He knew that the right thing to do was to pause and linger in the emptiness, stillness, and silence. In Bruce's own words, "I knew this beautiful and memorable moment of silence belonged to the patient and his lover." Everyone else in that hospital room knew the same and stood silently around the old soldier in his bed. After a silence lasting a few eternal minutes, the patient softly whispered his gratitude to Bruce.

The reason I offer this case to you is to illustrate the difference between doing and being. The brilliance and beauty of what Bruce accomplished were not in his doing. It was much more than the singing of the song. For if that was it, then we can invent yet another school of therapy practice and call it "choral therapy." But to do so would miss the point. It was not about the technique or the "intervention" of the song. To turn what Bruce did into another technique to be separated and formalized into another system and procedure would be foolish as Zhuangzi (1998) warned us in the following parable about absurdity:

> The emperor of the Southern Sea was Lickety, the emperor of the Northern Sea was Split, and the emperor of the Center was Wonton. Lickety and Split often met each other in the land of Wonton, and Wonton treated them very well. Wanting to repay Wonton's kindness, Lickety and Split said, "All people have seven holes for seeing, hearing, eating, and breathing. Wonton alone lacks them. Let's try boring some holes for him." So every

> day they bored one hole, and on the seventh day Wonton died. (p. xxxix)

Thus, the training question that I ask my students is, "How much and what part of yourself are you willing to offer and share with your clients?" Will you offer them your expert opinions, your techniques, your solutions, or your brilliant interpretations? Or will you offer them your being? The healing factor, in this case, was not the song. The song was but the vehicle for Bruce to enter into a deep encounter with the patient, where one being touches another and draws in the rest of the universe. In such moments, on the outside it appears as if nothing has changed. Yet, it is also in such moments that we know that everything changes. Good therapy consists of such brief and yet eternal moments. And if we are to bring our clients into such moments of healing, then it requires us to cultivate our beings and be attuned to and surrender ourselves to the Tao, a source of wisdom that is much greater than ourselves.

Bruce could never have intentionally prepared for that transformative moment. It is inconceivable for one to prepare a song before entering into that hospital room. All he could do is to remain empty, bracketed, naive, open, and attuned, trusting that he had been preparing all his life for such moments. Indeed, the song arose out of his own lived experience with loss and separation. As a supervisor, how could I prepare Bruce for such moments? With someone as talented as Bruce, I kept reminding myself to get out of his way and let go of my desire to teach and supervise. It was important for me to empty myself and practice non-action, trusting that life, existence, and the Tao would reveal itself to Bruce if I could simply practice Wu Wei and learn to lose myself in the ways of the Tao. In much of our year-long supervision, my job was simply to bear witness to Bruce's creativity and anchor him by giving occasional reminders not to be over-zealous. Bruce was such a healing presence because of the deep trust he had in himself. His willingness to bare his soul and share that song with the initial reticent patient amid such a chaotic environment was a testament to his courage as a healer. Like the old swimmer in Zhuangzi's parable, Bruce was following what was innate. He was in his element swimming through the rapids of the modern Chinese healthcare system. It would have been foolish for me to practice anything but the Wu Wei of non-interference.

Now, won't you use your imagination and join Bruce in that hospital room encounter that he so graciously shared with me. And to help with the journey, here are the translated lyrics to the Chinese song that Bruce sang to the dying man. Once you read the words, you will understand the longing of this man to return to the grave and how Bruce helped to transport him there.

Original Chinese	English Translation
你 说 你 最 爱 丁 香 花	Your favorite flower is Lilac
因 为 你 的 名字 就 是 它	For this is your name
多 么 忧 郁 的 花	A melancholic flower
多 愁 善 感 的 人 啊	A sentimental you
当 花 儿 枯 萎 的 时 候	Upon your wilting
当 画 面 定 格 的 时 候	Time stood still
多 么 嫩 的 花	Such a tender and lovely flower
却 躲 过 风 吹 雨 打	Battered by the wind and rain
飘 啊 摇 啊 的 一 生	Fluttering through life
多 少 美 丽 编 织 的 梦 啊	Weaving dreams, one after another
就 这 样 匆 匆 你 走 了	Hastily, you left
留 给 我 一 生 牵 挂	Leaving me a lifetime of reminiscence
那 坟 前 开 满 鲜 花	Fresh flowers blooming at your graveside
是 你 多 么 渴 望 的 美 啊	the beauty you longed for
你 看 那 满 山 遍 野	A mountain of blossoms
你 还 觉 得 孤 单 吗	Are you lonely still?
你 听 那 有 人 在 唱	Listen, a serenade,
那 首 你 最 爱 的 歌 谣 啊	your favorite ballad
尘 世 间 多 少 繁 芜	Worry no more
从 此必 再 牵 挂	about the needless cares of the world
(Repeat all x 1)	

日子里栽满丁香花
开满制胜美丽的鲜花
我在这里陪着她
一生一世保护她

Lilac, my daily companion
My beautiful,
blossoming Lilac
I’m here with you
to protect you now and
forever

Chapter 4

Tracy's Story: Steadiness in the Midst of Chaos

Tracy, like Bruce, was another talented and compassionate student under my supervision. She was one of a small minority of students who intentionally chose to conduct her clinical training at a palliative care center. Most students stayed far away from such depressing placements, thinking like the servant in the following story in Frankl's (1985) book *Man's Search for Meaning.* A rich Persian master was walking in his garden when one of his servants rushed up to him and cried that he had just encountered and was threatened by Death. He begged his master to show mercy and lend him his fastest horse so he could make haste and flee. The master granted the servant's wish and the servant wasted no time in fleeing to Tehran. Later in the day, the master himself met Death and inquired why Death had threatened his servant? Death replied, "I did not threaten him. I only showed my astonishment upon finding him still here when I planned to meet him in Tehran this evening."

Tracy was wise and courageous perhaps knowing that all of us are on our way to Tehran. Running away from the inevitability of death will bring us closer to Tehran before the evening. During the practicum, Tracy worked hard to earn the trust of a family whose father was dying. She earned this trust through respect and receptive listening. Tracy had a wonderful relationship with her grandfather and enjoyed listening to her grandfather's stories. She naturally relished taking on the role of the devoted daughter or granddaughter "sitting at the feet" of the elder patients in the waiting room of the palliative care center. She earned trust by humbling herself and realizing that much of what she had to offer was achieved by taking on a lower receptive position rather than the higher position of knowledge. In other words, Tracy had to once again empty herself in order to receive. Tracy realized that at the end of life, many elders crave significance and need people to listen to their stories as they reflect and attempt to make sense of their lives. Tracy knew intuitively of the final developmental task of integrity versus despair, proposed by developmental psychologist Erik Erikson. She was there not only to listen but to help patients achieve integrity as they face the end of their lives. The wisdom and compassion of Tracy's humility and receptiveness are described by Lao Tzu (1995) in verse 15 of the *Tao Te Ching*:

> The ancient Masters were profound and subtle.
> Their wisdom was unfathomable.
> There is no way to describe it;
> all we can describe is their appearance.
>
> They were careful
> as someone crossing an iced-over stream.
> Alert as a warrior in enemy territory.
> Courteous as a guest.
> Fluid as melting ice.
> Shapable as a block of wood.
> Receptive as a valley.
> Clear as a glass of water.
>
> Do you have the patience to wait
> till your mud settles and the water is clear?
> Can you remain unmoving
> till the right action arises by itself?
>
> The Master doesn't seek fulfillment.
> Not seeking, not expecting,
> she is present, and can welcome all things.

Flexibility and Humility

Just as Tracy humbled herself, I, too, was humbled by Tracy's wisdom and learned a number of valuable lessons from her. One of the things I learned as a supervisor for the palliative training site was that we needed to be flexible. During my clinical training, I was ingrained with the inviolability of confidentiality, the sanctity of the therapeutic room, the discipline of time management, and the competence of being knowledgeable and in control—the pillars of psychotherapy, and for good reason. However, Tracy taught me about the importance of adaptability and the need to be flexible for Tracy did all of her work in the crowded waiting room of the palliative care center where there was little to no privacy. Since that time, in addition to teaching my supervisees about the pillars of psychotherapy, I also urge them not to be overly rigid as verse 76 (excerpts) of the Tao Te Ching states: "When life begins we are tender and weak. When life ends we are stiff and rigid. All things, including the grass and trees, are soft and pliable in life dry and brittle in death. So soft and supple are the companions of life, while the stiff and unyielding are the companions of death" (Lao Tzu, 2003, p. 89).

Flexibility also needs to be paired with humility. A private and comfortable interview room was available for use. However, if Tracy were to insist upon carrying out her conversations in the safety of the interview room, nothing would have been accomplished. Patient and their families made the trek to the palliative care center in order to see doctors, not therapists. They looked to the medical authorities for comfort and care for their physical pain. There was not much openness for the comfort of their psychological pain, especially in the open setting of a public hospital waiting room. In fact, many would actively distance themselves from the stigma of talking to a psychologist. Therefore, Tracy had to tend to hidden psychological needs that were often actively denied. Tracy had to be proactive and meet the patients where they were at. And the waiting room was where the psychological analgesic was to be delivered. However, the waiting room offered no safety or privacy. Conversations and even tears were shared openly next to other waiting patients. Furthermore, the conversation could be interrupted at any time because one never knew when it was the patient's turn to see the physician. Indeed, often the "sessions" were short, nowhere close to the magical one-hour duration. Talk about humility and the lack of control. Finally, any follow-up sessions were typically tied to the patient's next appointment with the physician. Tracy was certainly happy to set up follow-up sessions with the patients, but logistically it was difficult for most patients to make the trek to the hospital. Each appointment often required the aid of family members, who had to take time off work to accompany the patients. Psychological comfort was not foremost on the patients' minds, despite all the compassion Tracy offered. Humility, flexibility, emptiness, patience, and persistence was what Tracy was developing amid such challenges. Tracy and I were learning about Zhuangzi's lesson of the usefulness of being useless discussed in the previous chapter.

So how can the patients and their families open up in such an unregulated setting? Yet, open up they did. Truth be told, the majority of the patients chose only to exchange short pleasantries with Tracy while waiting for their turn to see their doctors. However, some families did choose to open up and take in Tracy's care. A few families chose to share deeply of their pain and anxiety in the brief encounters that took place in that waiting room. The story of this chapter centers upon one such family, which consisted of the father, mother, and teenage son. Tracy encountered this family near the end of her year-long training period and did not know if she would be able to accompany this family till the death of the father. The day I received Tracy's call was the day of the father's passing.

Faith and Trust

Tracy called me while I was riding the subway and asked me for any last advice I could offer before she went to accompany the mother and son at the father's deathbed. Tracy had earned enough trust with the family to be invited to be part of such an honorable moment. Though looking forward to it, for Tracy and I knew that these are the enduring, memorable times in one's life and clinical work, we both also felt at a loss as to what to do. What would you tell Tracy as a supervisor? What advice would you offer? The call from the family had come out of nowhere, and both Tracy and I were similarly surprised and taken aback.

Knowing that I needed to slow things down, I first told Tracy that I needed to get off the subway and find a quiet place where I could call her back. This also allowed me to buy some time to think of something helpful to pass along to Tracy on her way to the hospital. What came to mind was something I had read from a book about death and dying at the time. The author said that auditory and tactile sensations are the last senses to go—that even when patients are unconscious they may be able to hear and feel what you say or do. Amid my helplessness, this was the best that I could offer at the moment. At the same time, I also repeated a consistent theme in our supervision. I encouraged Tracy to once again be open to learning from her clients and that this was a rare opportunity for learning. Tracy thanked me and entered the hospital.

How did I do? What do you think Tracy needed? If I could do this a second time, how would you advise me to "supervise" Tracy?

Having the benefit of hindsight and more time for reflection, I realized later what Tracy and the client both needed. This is the concept of parallel process. The idea that what happens between supervisor and supervisee often parallels what takes place between the client and therapist. Looking back, what I realized was that what Tracy was seeking from me was not simply advice. For what "advice," "to-do's" could I squeeze into such a short phone call? What Tracy needed from me—what students often need from their supervisors, what children need from their parents—is faith and assurance. What Tracy needed from me were my presence and companionship. She needed the sense that I was with her, that I believed in her, and that I had faith that she was up to the task. When I shared Tracy's story at a later workshop, a physician spoke of a similar experience. She shared the anxiety she felt prior to giving an important talk in front of a large audience. In the midst of her anxiety, she called her mentor only to be directed to his voicemail. However, upon hearing his recorded, professional-sounding voice, she immediately felt calm and connected and went on to deliver a successful talk. On some level, Tracy simply needed to hear my voice and know that I had faith in her and was there to back her up. She needed to know that she was not alone. Thus, if I could have had a second chance with Tracy, I'd tell her that she had been courageously present for the family throughout their journey thus far. She had been whole-hearted in her work, and her compassion was why the mother had called and extended the invitation to join them in their time of need. "Go forth Tracy and do what you do. I have faith in you!" I offer these words based on the following passage from Daniel Gottlieb (2010), an author who became a quadriplegic as the result of a freak accident:

> What clients need is trust that they have the resilience, in themselves, to meet the unknown, to experience it, and to survive. They need to learn the lessons that only nature—not his parents—could teach him. What they needed from their parents was what all children needed from their parents: the faith that they can endure adversity. When a child does not have a parents' faith, they experience the parents' anxiety. And in time, the child comes to experience him/herself as fragile in the face of a difficult world. As a result, the child never gets a chance to "toughen up."
>
> Resilience cannot be taught. It is to be nurtured by faith. It's something that clients already have inside. I don't know about you, but all the wisdom I've acquired has come from adversity,

> pain, suffering, loss, and some really stupid decisions. All of these things have caused me great suffering. I have learned that every time I suffer, I recover. And over time, that knowledge has turned to faith. Now I have faith that when I face adversity, somehow I'll be okay. It might not be the outcome I would prefer, but I have faith that I will be okay with what is. (p. 58)

So Tracy arrived at the hospital and walked into a quiet and somber room except for the mother, who was wailing away because she did not know how to deal with the imminent death of her husband. The pain was too much to bear. Her relatives were there trying to lend support but felt quite helpless and had given up trying to comfort the mother. Imagine the scene that Tracy faced. She was the outsider amidst an overwhelmed, hysterical mother in the center of a crowd of helpless relatives. Tracy later informed me that, like the relatives, she also felt desperate and helpless.

However, Tracy was resilient, and in the midst of the despair came inspiration and creativity. For we are like olives: only when we are crushed do we yield what is best in us (The Talmud, Hebrew Book of Wisdom). Tracy emptied and calmed herself, reflected inwardly, attuning herself to the moment and her lived experience. She practiced what Zhuangzi (1998) described as fasting of the mind, referred to earlier in Chapter 2, on humanistic education. Tracy looked deeply into the void, dwelling in emptiness; she avoided the galloping while sitting, which often occurs when we are overcome with anxiety amid helplessness. Continuing with the words of Zhuangzi (1998):

> To eliminate one's footsteps by not walking is easy, but to walk without touching the ground is hard. If you are impelled by human feelings, it is easy to be false. I've only heard of creatures that fly with wings, never of creatures that fly with non-wings. I've only heard of people knowing things through awareness, never of people knowing things through unawareness. Observe the void—the empty emits a pure light. Good fortune lies in stopping when it is time to stop. If you do not stop, this is called "galloping while sitting." Let your senses communicate within and rid yourself of the machinations of the mind. Then even ghosts and spirits will take shelter with you, not to mention men. This is how the myriad things are transformed. (p. 33)

Hearing the Unheard

Immersing herself in the ways of Wu Wei, Tracy walked without touching the ground, flew with non-wings, and became aware of what previously was unaware. She learned, like the prince from the story below, to hear the unheard. A father sent a young prince to a Chinese master to learn how to become a good ruler. The master began by sending the young prince to spend a year alone in the forest. Upon his return, the master asked the prince to describe what he heard. The prince told of cuckoos singing, leaves rusting, hummingbirds humming, crickets chirping, grass blowing, bees buzzing, and the whispering and hollering of the wind. The master acknowledged this and sent the prince back to the forest to listen for more. The prince did as he was told but was perplexed as to what the master was talking about. After several days and nights, he began to hear the unheard. Upon his return, the prince reported to the master of hearing the sounds of flowers opening, grass drinking the morning dew, and the warming of the earth by the rays of the sun. The master nodded.

> "To hear the unheard," he said, "is a necessary discipline to be a good ruler. For only when a ruler has learned to listen closely to the people's hearts, hearing their feelings uncommunicated, pains unexpressed, and complaints not spoken of, can he hope to inspire confidence in the people, understand when something is wrong, and meet the true needs of his citizens." (Jackson & Delehanty, 2013, p. 99)

In other words, Tracy assessed the situation and listened to the void the way the little girl in the story below wanted to be listened to:

> A little girl came home from school with a drawing she'd made in class. She danced into the kitchen, where her mother was preparing dinner.
>
> "Mom, guess what?" she squealed, waving the drawing.
>
> Her mother never looked up. "What?" she said, tending to the pots.
>
> "Guess what?" the child repeated, waving the drawing.
>
> "What?" the mother said, tending to the plates.
>
> "Mom, you're not listening."
>
> "Sweetie, yes I am."

> "Mom," the child said, "You're not listening with your eyes!" (Albom, 2009, p. 75)

Amid the cacophony, Tracy stilled herself and asked herself a simple question, "I too am a wife. What would I need if I were my client?" The answer appeared soon thereafter from the depth of the void and Tracy's lived experience. Tracy remembered that it had been a long while since the couple was physically affectionate. She attuned to herself and realized that as a wife, what she treasured most was to be held. So gathering up courage, risking coming across like a fool, the outsider who had the least right to offer advice in that room, Tracy asked the mother if she would like to go and lie down next to her husband. In doing so, Tracy showed amazing steadiness in the midst of chaos described by Zhuangzi (1998) in the following parable:

> Yen Yuan inquired of Confucius, saying, "When I was crossing the gulf of Goblet Deep, the ferryman handled the boat like a spirit. I asked him about it, saying, 'Can handling a boat be learned?' 'Yes," said he, 'good swimmers can learn quickly. As for divers, they can handle a boat right away without ever having seen one.' I asked him why this was so, but he didn't tell me. I ventured to ask you what you think he meant."
>
> "A good swimmer can learn quickly because he forgets about the water," said Confucius. "As for a diver being able to handle a boat right away without ever having seen one, it's because he regards the watery depth as if they were a mound and the capsizing of a boat as if it were the rolling back of a carriage. Capsizing and rolling back could unfold a myriad times before him without affecting his heart, so he is relaxed wherever he goes. He who competes for a piece of tile displays all of his skill; he who competes for a belt buckle gets nervous; he who competes for gold gets flustered. His skill is still the same, but there is something that distracts him and causes him to focus on externals. Whoever focuses on externals will be clumsy inside." (p. 177)

In addition to displaying amazing steadiness in the midst of chaos, Tracy also drew upon her own lived experience as a mother. She was able to empathize with the mother because she, too, was deeply invested in life, in living out her existence, similarly to Master Chan from the story of Boya's Lesson with the Zither below. Though I could introduce existential psychology to Tracy, it was Life itself that gave Tracy the wisdom to care for the mother as she did:

> Boya was a talented musician from the Spring and Autumn period (722–481 B. C.) in Ancient China.
>
> According to history passed down from various families, Boya began a zither apprenticeship with Master Chan. Yet, after three years, Boya was intriguingly unable to express tenors of melancholy through his performances. Master Chan informed Boya that while he could teach Boya how to play the zither, he was unable to instruct him as to how to feel. Thus, Master Chan brought Boya to the East Sea to study with Fangzichun, Master Chan's teacher, who inspired many to reconnect with their own emotions. Upon arrival at Penglai Hill of the East Sea, Master Chan instructed Boya to continue with his practice while he went to fetch his Master.
>
> Ten days pass since the pilgrimage and Master Chan has yet to return. Boya begins to feel hopeless and lonely, accompanied only by sorrowful cries of the seagulls and the endless raging of the sea. It was at that point that Boya felt the breath of heaven intimating Master Chan's intentions to teach Boya about Wu Wei, sentiments, and sensitivities. It was then that Boya composed the piece Narcissus《水仙操》for the zither. Thus it was said that "Horses will pause from their grazing upon Boya's music; if even birds and the beasts are inspired, how about the rest of us?"
>
> Perhaps this can be considered one of the earliest understandings of the word "empathy" (though literal translation of the word 移情 is the transfer of feelings, evoking current understanding of transference in psychological circles).
>
> Boya was inspired to compose Narcissus because he was intentionally left on the deserted island and became aware of and touched by the turbulent sea and the sorrowful cries of the seagulls. Therefore, empathy can be evoked through or perhaps requires encounters with nature such that one becomes integrated with one's surroundings and achieves harmony between heaven and earth that is of the highest order. This cannot help but explain that music appreciation begins with a deep recognition of the unity between man and nature and the understanding that the highest realm of art is harmoniously

> integrated with nature and intimately interconnected with humanity.[1]

Being Fully Present: In the Zone

How did Tracy know when to intervene? A difficult question to answer. It's like asking how did the fruit know it was ripe and time to drop from the tree branch? How did the diver know when to initiate her dive? Tracy was in the zone, and the interesting fact about being in the zone is that "it really cannot be described accurately because at the moment you are in that state, the ability to describe is not present. After you are out of the state, you may try to remember what it was like" (Galloway, 1997, p. 98).

Being in the zone means being fully present. We all desire to dwell in the zone and be in control of its arrival. But being in the zone is a gift. It is not a gift you can demand of yourself, but one you can ask for by putting forth a Wu Wei sort of effort, a non-action sort of action, an effort characterized not by force but by letting go of conscious control. As one learns to trust that unconscious force, the desire for conscious control quiets and the way of the Tao becomes more conscious, more present; enjoyment increases and the gifts are more apt to flow.

> If you are willing to give credit where credit is due and not think you "know" how to do it, the gifts are apt to be more frequent and sustainable. The gift comes at its own timing, when I am ready for it—humble, respectful, not expecting it, somehow placing myself lower than it, not above it. Then when the moment is right, it comes, and I can enjoy the absence of Self 1 thought and the presence of joy. I like it a lot. Grab for it, and it will squirt away like a slippery bar of soap. Take it for granted, and you will be distracted and lose it. I used to think that whatever was present in that state would leave me, was ephemeral. Now I know that it is always there and it is only I who leave. When I look at a young child I realize it is there all the time. As the child grows, there is more to distract the mind, and it is harder to recognize. But it, Self 2, may be the only thing

---

[1] Excerpts from *History of Qin,* translated by Mark Yang and retrieved from the following Chinese website on March 14, 2019: https://mp.weixin.qq.com/s/gN3O2woXWczZbNHi5hKL3Q

> which has been there and will be there your entire life. Thoughts and thinking come and go, but the child self, the true self, is there and will be there as long as our breath is. To enjoy it, to appreciate it, is the gift of focus. (Galloway, 1997, p. 99)[2]

Timing was everything and Tracy was patient while in the zone and being fully present in the room. Lao Tzu would have praised Tracy for remaining unmoving until the right action became apparent. "Therapy requires good timing. Timing is inevitably ruined when the therapist feels a need to fill in space, to do something just to produce more visible action." (Johanson & Kurtz, 1991, p. 55). The process is like giving birth. The midwife (think back to Socrates) is the one with the experience and sense of when to take action and when to relax. "When something is developing organically, the next right action inevitably suggests itself, as does the right rhythm for acting. Much of therapy is an act of trust. When things seem muddy, we can be patient if we believe they will eventually become clear" (Johanson & Kurtz, 1991, p. 55).

Stillness and Going Nowhere

Tracy's inspired intervention arose out of her emptiness and stillness. Like the prince in the story above, Tracy needed to slow down and still herself if she were to hear the deep voice of her empathy. A most challenging practice amid chaos. It is when we're able to still ourselves that we can achieve the calmness of mind necessary to be a healing presence. Sir William Osler, one of the fathers of modern medicine, is widely quoted as having said that objectivity is the essential quality of the true physician. However, Dr. Remen (2006), pointed out that what Osler actually said is different and far more profound. Dr. Remen taught that the original quote was in Latin and the Latin word Osler used was *aequanimatas*, which is usually translated as "objectivity." But aequanimatas means "calmness of mind," "equanimity," or "inner peace." Interestingly, Sir William Osler's quote has been understood to promote objectivity, which connotes distance when, in fact, it has to do more with calmness of mind and inner peace, which implies more nearness and deeper subjectivity.

Similarly, Pico Iyer (2014), a journalist and novelist who has traveled the world, found his most meaningful experiences while

---

[2] Self 1, as denoted by the author, can be understood as conscious control while Self 2 is more akin to an unconscious, trusting part of ourselves.

paradoxically going nowhere. In his book *The Art of Stillness: Adventures in Going Nowhere,* he reflected that going nowhere is that which makes sense of everywhere else. Not long ago, it was movement and access to information that was our greatest luxury; nowadays, it is the liberation from information, the chance to be still that is luxurious. Put another way, Chang Ch'ao stated, "Only those who take leisurely what the people of the world are busy about can be busy about what the people of the world take leisurely" (as cited in Lin, 2008, Preface). Movement becomes more meaningful within the context of stillness. "It's only when you stop moving that you can be moved in some far deeper way" (Iyer, 2014, p. 11). Paradoxically, retreats are the best way to advance. The trips that we've taken become more insightful and memorable when we have the chance to reflect upon them in our moments of stillness. It is the meanings that we imbue, not the places we visit, that ultimately tell us where we stand. Stillness and going nowhere is not about austerity as much as about getting back in touch with oneself. Iyer's writings elucidate the meaning of Zhuangzi's admonition for us to find wisdom, knowledge in the "palace of Nowhere." It is in this place of emptiness where the Tao is to be found:

> Tao is Great in all things,
> Complete in all, Universal in all,
> Whole in all. These three aspects
> Are distinct, but the Reality is One.
>
> "Therefore come with me
> To the palace of Nowhere
> Where all the many things are One:
> There at last we might speak
> Of what has no limitation and no end.
>
> Come with me to the land of Non-Doing:
> What shall we there say – that Tao
> Is simplicity, stillness,
> Indifference, purity,
> Harmony and ease? All these names leave me indifferent
> For their distinctions have disappeared.
>
> My will is aimless there.
> If it is nowhere, how should I be aware of it?
> If it goes and returns, I know not

Where it has been resting. If it wander
Here and there, I know not where it will end.

The mind remains undetermined in the great Void.
Here the highest knowledge
Is unbounded. That which gives things
Their thusness cannot be delimited by thing.
(Merton, 2010, pp. 123–124)

Lao Tzu wrote about the same theme of emptiness and non-action at the beginning of the Tao Te Ching:

Tao Te Ching, Verse 2

Everyone recognizes beauty
  only because of ugliness
Everyone recognizes virtue
  only because of sin

Life and death are born together
Difficult and easy
Long and short
High and low—
  all these exist together
Sound and silence blend as one
Before and after arrive as one

The Sage acts without action
  And teaches without talking
All things flourish around him
  and he does not refuse any one of them
He gives but not to receive
He works but not for reward
He completes but not for results
He does nothing for himself in this passing world
  so nothing he does ever passes (Lao Tzi, 2003, p. 15)

Tao Te Ching, Verse 3

If you overesteem great men,
people become powerless.

If you overvalue possessions,
people begin to steal.

The Master leads
by emptying people's minds
and filling their cores,
by weakening their ambition
and toughening their resolve.
He helps people lose everything
they know, everything they desire,
and creates confusion
in those who think that they know.

Practice not-doing,
and everything will fall into place. (Lao Tzu, 1995)

Perhaps Rumi (n.d.) said it best when he wrote:

Silence is the
Language of God,
All else is
Poor translation

Tracy's inspired suggestion in the midst of chaos is akin to the poet's struggle to make non-being, be. Great poetry is born in silence. In his book *Poetry and Experience*, Archibald MacLeish quotes a Chinese Poet: "We poets struggle with Non-being and force it to yield Being. We knock upon silence for an answering music" (as cited in May, 1994, p. 79). Rollo May elaborates on this eloquent and mysterious process of creating poetry:

> "The Being" which the poem is to contain derives from "Non-being," not from the poet. And the "music" which the poem is to own comes not from us who makes the poem but from silence; comes an *answer* to our knock. The verbs are eloquent: "struggle," "knock." The poet's labor is to struggle with the meaninglessness and silence of the world until he can force it to mean; until he can make the silence answer and the Non-being be. It is a labor which undertakes to "know" the world not by exegesis or demonstration or proofs but directly, as a man knows apple in the mouth. (p. 79)

Let's return to Tracy's story. Tracy's invitation to lie next to her husband shocked the wife out of her wailing stupor. She stared wide-eyed at Tracy and asked innocently, "May I?" Tracy nodded reassuringly thus "granting permission," performing one of the most basic tasks of a grief counselor. The mother, who then stopped crying, slowly walked over to her unconscious husband and snuggled up next to him in bed. After a while, she began whispering to him. She told a beautiful tale that was Tracy's eternal reward. Tracy told me later that this was the most beautiful lesson she learned from that evening. The mother told the husband of her gratefulness to him for staying by her all these years. It turns out that the mother suffered from bi-polar disorder and had been on medication for over 20 years. She poured her heart out and told her husband how much she loved and appreciated him for not abandoning her. The ironic thing, of course, is that the mother was whispering this as the husband was slipping away from her. Even so, Zhuangzi (1998) reminds us again that, "Resins may be consumed when they are used for fuel, but the fire they transmit knows no end" (p. 28).

Tracy's gift from that evening, and my lesson once again, is that life and death are simultaneous and equiprimordial. The following quotes came flooding back to me ever more powerfully:

> "In the last analysis, it is our conception of death which decides our answers to all the questions that life puts to us." Dag Hammarskjold (n.d.), Noble Peace Prize Winner, Secretary-General of the United Nations
>
> "Ever has it been that love knows not its own depth until the hour of separation." (Gibran, 2015, Chapter 1, para. 52)
>
> When you part from your friend, you grieve not. For that which you love in him may be clearer in his absence, as the mountain to the climber is clearer from the plain." (Gibran, 2015, Chapter 19, para. 9)[3]

---

[3] Kahlil Gibran's poem from *The Prophet (2015)* is now part of the public domain.

A Priceless Gift

The husband died later that evening. His family and extended family were with him till the end. So was Tracy. After a period of being with the body, the family ended their vigil, got up, and began to leave. Yet, Tracy remained attuned to the moment. She noticed that the teenage son had been sitting quietly in the corner by himself for most of the evening. Courageously, she once again took charge, gently ushering the family out and inviting the boy to spend some time alone with his father. She then drew the curtain around the bed in the hospital room, creating a sacred space and time between father and son. After some time, the boy came out, and they all went home.

What Tracy was able to accomplish for the mother and son was priceless. It helped me to better understand the famous Biblical parable where Jesus was anointed by an unnamed woman with precious nard from a priceless alabaster vial. The woman was chastised harshly by those present for wasting the perfume, which could have been sold for more than a year's wages and the money given to the poor. This made a lot of sense for Jesus had a heart for the poor. So in my first reading, I thought Jesus would gently concur with a rebuke while offering benevolent understanding to the woman for her beautiful intentions. Yet, I was totally surprised by Jesus' response:

> "Leave her alone," said Jesus. "Why are you bothering her? She has done a beautiful thing to me. The poor you will always have with you, and you can help them any time you want. But you will not always have me. She did what she could. She poured perfume on my body beforehand to prepare for my burial. Truly I tell you, wherever the gospel is preached throughout the world, what she has done will also be told, in memory of her. (Mark 14: 6–9)

Through lived experience, through facing the death of my father, I've come to a deeper understanding of the meaning of such priceless moments—precious, eternal moments that Tracy captured for mother and son. And how quickly such moments pass uncaptured and end up being lifelong regrets. In this matter, I write from personal experience for I wish Tracy had been there to do the same for me at the time of my father's death. My father passed away in the United States, and I rushed back from China to be with him. Unfortunately, he was out of conscious awareness by the time I arrived. He passed away on a Saturday evening, and I was called to view his body and be with him one final time the following morning. His body was brought out of the morgue on a stainless-steel stretcher. Everything was cold and antiseptic, matching my mood at the moment. The social worker encouraged me to take as much time as I needed and settled on the couch in the back of the viewing room. I touched my father's bald head and found him to as frigid as I was numb. What was there to say to a father who offered little in terms of words or emotional expression? Far too often, only a few awkward sentences were exchanged between us during my frequent visits throughout his previous hospital stays. An hour of silence after sixteen-hour roundtrips on the road. Painful silence between a Chinese father and his son. So what was I to say during our last moment together? Years of things unsaid squeezed into a few precious moments. A wave of sadness arose in me, but I could not bring myself to cry in the presence of the social worker. I could have asked her to give me a few private moments with my father. Surely she would have complied. Yet I could not utter such simple words. My disdain for inconveniencing others outweighed the permission I needed to allow myself to grieve. A lifelong regret of mine. Where was Tracy when I needed her?

It is much easier to teach than to practice. I'm still learning to show compassion to myself for failing to avail for myself of what I've taught others on numerous occasions. We are human, all too human. I realize once again that time stops for no one. But, fortunately, the regrets of my past can be meaningful lessons for future clients and supervisees. This is how I make meaning of my loss. Who is the teacher/supervisor and who is the student/supervisee anyway? When it comes to facing the existential givens, once again we are all fellow travelers.

Tracy journeyed with this family from anticipatory grief into grief. She was rewarded with the honor of being allowed to be with the family in their hour of need. Tracy was able to meet with the boy separately on several occasions after the father's death. The boy did not take up offers to meet with the school counselor nor did he talk to the teachers about his grief. Yet, he agreed to meet with Tracy, and they had their final goodbye in a restaurant of his choice at the end of Tracy's training placement. It was a proper validation of Tracy's courage and compassion—a validation most powerfully offered to Tracy as only a teenage boy can in his understated way. Once again, my role was merely that of a witness, a student, paralleling the role that Tracy took on with her clients; being reminded again that it is our courage and not our titles that earn us the right to be therapists or supervisors. The invitation and entry into this family's life, particularly the life of the teenage boy, was the validation of Tracy's gift as a therapist. What a wonderful endorsement at the completion of Tracy's training placement. The boy and her mother taught Tracy about life and death. They bolstered her confidence and furthered Tracy's development as a therapist and person in much more powerful ways than I. Tracy bore witness to their pain. I bore witness to Tracy's growth.

What we saw from Tracy was a beautiful act of creation. Where was the source of this creation? Guided by Lao Tzu (1995) and the end of verse one of the Tao Te Ching, my answer to that question is that the source came out of despair: "Darkness within darkness, the gateway to all understanding." An inspiration that arose from Tracy's courage to face helplessness and not shy away. It also came from Tracy's lived experience. Through Tracy's experience, both her and I learned once again that life and death are interdependent, just as are with joy and sorrow.

> Your joy is your sorrow unmasked.
> And the selfsame well from which your laughter rises was oftentimes filled with your tears.
> And how else can it be?
> The deeper that sorrow carves into your being, the more joy you can contain.
> Is not the cup that holds your wine the very cup that was burned in the potter's oven?
> And is not the lute that soothes your spirit the very wood that was hollowed with knives?
> When you are joyous, look deep into your heart and you shall find it is only that which has given you sorrow that is giving you joy.
> When you are sorrowful, look again in your heart and you shall see that in truth you are weeping for that which has been your delight.
>
> Some of you say, "Joy is greater than sorrow," and others say, "Nay, sorrow is the greater."
> But I say unto you, they are inseparable.
> Together they come, and when one sits, alone with you at your board, remember that the other is asleep upon your bed.
> Verily you are suspended like scales between your sorrow and your joy.
> Only when you are empty are you at standstill and balanced.

> When the treasure-keeper lifts you to weigh his gold and his silver, needs must your joy or your sorrow rise or fall. (Gibran, 2015, Chapter 8, para 1)

Tracy gave out of her lived-experience in life. I could not hope to squeeze in enough advice to help Tracy as she prepared to walk those last few steps with this family. Nevertheless, I could inspire and liberate. What assured me in terms of preparedness is that in many ways, Tracy and I had been preparing all during our nine months of supervision up to that point for those last few steps. The preparation was not linear. It was cumulative. What Tracy brought into that room with her was the accumulation of her life experiences and the accumulation of the professional and personal transformations that had taken place during our nine months of supervision up to that point. I'd be foolish not to encourage Tracy to tap into all that experience. How much could I give to Tracy compared to all that she already contained within? More than teaching, my role as a supervisor was to help Tracy trust what was natural and innate and dwell in the mystery of the Tao. Recall Dag Hammarskjold's quote above that it is the conception of death that gives us the answers to all of life's questions. The meaning or fruits of our training is manifested at such times. Tracy and I could not have planned for the moments that Tracy created with the family. What we could do was to align ourselves with the Way of the Tao as described by both Lao Tzu and Zhuangzi in their writings below.

Tao Te Ching, Verse 27

A good traveler has no fixed plans
and is not intent upon arriving.
A good artist lets his intuition
lead him wherever it wants.
A good scientist has freed himself of concepts
and keeps his mind open to what is.

Thus the Master is available to all people
and doesn't reject anyone.
He is ready to use all situations
and doesn't waste anything.
This is called embodying the light.

What is a good man but a bad man's teacher?

What is a bad man but a good man's job?
If you don't understand this, you will get lost,
however intelligent you are.
It is the great secret. (Lao Tzu, 1995)

The Master Book/Butcher (庖丁解牛)

A cook was cutting up an ox for Lord Wenhui.

Wherever
His hand touched,
His shoulder leaned
His foot stopped,
His knee nudged

the flesh would fall away with a swishing sound. Each slice of the cleaver was right in tune, zip zap! He danced in rhythm to "The Mulberry Grove," moved in concert with the strains of "The Managing Chief."

"Ah, wonderful" said Lord Wenhui, "That skill can attain such heights!"

The cook put down his cleaver and responded, "What your servant loves is the Way, which goes beyond mere skill. When I first began to cut oxen, what I saw was nothing but whole oxen. After three years, I no longer saw whole oxen. Today, I meet the ox with my spirit rather than looking at it with my eyes. My sense organs stop functioning and my spirit moves as it pleases.

In accord with the natural grains, I slice at the great crevices, lead the blade through the great cavities. Following its inherent structure, I never encounter the slightest obstacle even where the veins and arteries come together or where the ligaments and tendons join, much less from obvious big bones. A good cook changes his cleaver once a year because he chops. An ordinary cook changes his cleaver once a month because he hacks. Now I've been using my cleaver for nineteen years and have cut up thousands of oxen with it, but the blade is still as fresh as though it had just come from the grindstone. Between the joints there are spaces, but the edge of the blade has no thickness. Since I am inserting something without any thickness into an empty space, there will certainly be lots of room for the blade to play around in. That's why the blade is still as fresh as though it had come from the grindstone. Nonetheless, whenever I come to a complicated spot and see that it will be difficult to handle, I cautiously restrain myself, focus my vision, and slow my motion. With an imperceptible movement of the cleaver, plop! And the flesh is already separated, like a clump of earth collapsing to the ground. I stand there holding the cleaver in my hand, look all around me with complacent satisfaction, then I wipe off the cleaver and store it away."

"Wonderful!" said Lord Wenhui. "From hearing the words of the cook, I have learned how to nourish life." (Zhuangzi, 1998, pp. 26–27)

Chapter 5

Petrus's Story: Companionship in the Midst of Suffering

The Power of Companionship

I was conducting a workshop in Singapore when an earnest student asked, "You talked a lot about the healing power of companionship, but how exactly does companionship help when it comes to pain and suffering?" I've accepted the "truth" that companionship is a powerful antidote for existential pain and suffering but it's been a while since I've pondered and had to explain why. The question from this "beginner's mind" challenged me to reflect deeper upon pain and the healing nature of companionship.

My reflections began with a deeper look into the nature of pain. In his book, *Pain, The Gift Nobody Wants,* Dr. Paul Brand (1993) explores the purpose and value of physical pain. Dr. Brand explains that though the body has involuntary reflexes that move us quickly away from pain, it is this feeling of unpleasantness that rouses and compels us to attend to and act upon the problem that is causing the pain. The pain also helps to imprint the experience deeply into our memory, serving as future protection. Thus, Dr. Brand urges us to develop gratitude in the face of pain. We may not desire the experience of pain, but we can be grateful for the system of pain perception. This brings to mind the famous saying by Ben Franklin (n.d.), "That which hurts, also instructs." Also, from the Talmud (n.d.), "For we are like olives: only when we are crushed do we yield what is best in us."

Rollo May (1981) adds that we convert pain into suffering in the mind. Similarly, Harold Kushner (2004) in the book *When Bad Things Happen to Good People,* gives the following example of the difference between pointless suffering and creative pain:

> Scientists have found ways of measuring the intensity of the pain we feel. They can measure the fact that a migraine headache hurts more than a skinned knee. And they have determined that two of the most painful things human being can experience are giving birth and passing a kidney stone. From a purely physical point of view, these two events both hurt equally, and hardly anything hurts more. But from a human point of view, the two are different. The pain of passing a kidney stone is simply pointless suffering, the result of a natural malfunction somewhere in our body. But the pain of giving birth is creative pain. It is pain that has meaning, pain that gives life, that lead to something. That is why the person who passes a kidney stone will usually say "I'd give anything not to have to go through that again," but the woman who has given birth to a child, like the runner or mountain climber who has driven his body to reach a goal, can transcend her pain and contemplate repeating the experience. (p. 72)

We need to make a distinction between acute pain and chronic pain. With acute pain, what we need to do is to look for immediate remedy. Nevertheless, our mindset still impacts how we perceive pain. My personal experience with this reality came at the expense of my knee. I learned about patient controlled analgesics (PCA) while recovering from my first knee surgery. For some reason, I had an allergic reaction to the anesthetic that was causing me to itch all over. Given that this was an infrequent occurrence, the nurse had to call the doctor to receive permission before administering medication that would alleviate my discomfort. The period of waiting dragged on because I was not in control of the situation. The waiting and helplessness that resulted from the lack of control exacerbated the discomfort. Fortunately, the medication in the form of a shot was eventually administered, and I was able to sleep through that first evening post-surgery. The second day, the nursing staff introduced the PCA to me. It came with a button that I could push to administer the analgesic whenever I needed it. Of course, there were upper dispensing limits so patients could not overdose. I was most thankful for this wonderful invention for it gave control, responsibility, and assurance back to me.

With time on my hands and being ever curious, I asked the head nurse about her experience with PCAs. She informed me that the nursing staff thought that the PCAs were a godsend because now they had one less task they needed to attend to during their busy shifts. I can imagine the task of having to administer analgesic shots to be stressful for the nursing staff as well. The wait was unpleasant for both the nursing staff and patients. Having control over someone else's pain is quite the responsibility. Vicarious pain is also pain. What's more interesting was when the head nurse shared about research findings showing that with PCA patients administered less pain medication to themselves when compared to the previous practice of doctor/nurse-administered analgesics. Depending on one's view of human nature, one might think that when left to their own devices, people would tend to abuse pain medications. It is this mistrust that leads to the strict control of pain medication within healthcare settings, and for good reason. However, the opposite is also true, as demonstrated by research. When given control and responsibility, the vast majority of patients will regulate their pain and choose to endure more pain instead of abusing analgesics.

Prior to modern research, people had long known that psychology plays a major role when it comes to pain perception and the tolerance of pain. To lessen the suffering of pain, Rollo May (1981) teaches that we need to make a crucial distinction between the pain of pain and the pain we create by our thoughts about the pain. Fear, anger, guilt, loneliness, and helplessness are all mental and emotional responses that can intensify pain. So, in working with pain, we can, of course, work at the lower levels of pain perception, using the tools of modern medicine such as medications and other procedures. At the same time, we can also work at the higher levels by modifying our outlook and attitude. And companionship is the "mechanism" through which we help our clients to endure and modify their outlook and attitudes toward pain and suffering.

Furthermore, fear and physical pain are synergistic. Severe pain produces the fear of pain, and that fear—any fear, but particularly the terror of severe physical suffering—increases the intensity of pain. While companionship cannot take away the physical pain, it can help to reduce the fear or even terror of that pain. This was my lived experience for I began experiencing a mild panic attack during my fourth knee surgery before the administration of anesthesia. It was not my first time around the block, so the panic attack was quite unexpected for me. The anesthesiologist needed to secure my arm to an adjoining section of the operating table. I began to feel claustrophobic and had a strong desire to fight back. It was at this point that an experienced and compassionate surgical nurse made eye contact and began explaining to me in a calm, soothing voice exactly what the team was doing step by step. I felt very alone in that cold, sterile environment and was beginning to recall movie scenes of execution by lethal injection. I was terrified. The surgical nurse's calming presence reminded me of Susan Sarandon's character in the movie *Dead Man Walking*, in which she told Sean Penn's character to gaze deeply into her eyes during the execution procedures. Through my lived experience, I came to a deeper understanding of the power of that scene and the comforting power of companionship in the midst of terror. Modern analgesics can help to manage the physical pain, but it is companionship that helps us with the higher levels of "pain management." It is companionship that gives validity to the experience that pain does not have to equal suffering. It is companionship that helps to share and lessen the burden of our clients' pain, thus giving credence to the aphorism "shared joy is twice the joy while shared grief is half the grief."

Dr. Brand makes one additional fascinating and critical observation. Because patients suffering from leprosy cannot feel their hands and feet, they feel like their extremities are just tools. Even though they can well see their hands and feet, they simply do not feel like a part of their body. They are not a part of "me." Thus, pain not only warns us and protects us; it also *unifies us.* Pain is an indispensable part of belongingness. In the same way that physical pain unifies our sense of having a body, we can conceive of the general experience of suffering as a unifying force that connects us with others. It is our vulnerability rather than our strength that connects us. This is perhaps the ultimate meaning behind our suffering. It is our suffering that is the most basic element that we share with others, the factor that unifies us with all living creatures. This is the reason why Brene Brown's (2010) talk on *The Power of Vulnerability* became one of the top 20 talks on TED. It is also why the Taoists favor the weak and undesirable for, ultimately, it is not our strength and put-togetherness but our pain and vulnerability that highlight our nobility and help us to connect with one another.

Courage and Creativity

So it is our suffering that unites us. It is also in unity or companionship that our pain need not be translated into suffering, and it is in companionship that our suffering can find its meaning. This beautiful interconnected principle was brought alive for me during one of my most challenging supervision sessions. It was also one of my finest supervisory sessions. The session did not start off very promisingly since, through parallel process, I was confronted with the same sense of helplessness as my supervisee. Nevertheless, amid despair came inspiration and beauty, which I would like to share with you.

Petrus is a classic example of a student for life (活到老， 学到老). He was a professor of social work at a local university with one doctorate already under his belt. Yet, his love for learning was such that he returned to school to pursue his second doctorate in clinical psychology. Naturally, when the staff at a local hospice where Petrus was conducting his practicum found out that they were working with a professor of social work, they quickly referred a number of their more challenging patients to his care, including one particular mother who was suffering greatly from both physical and psychological pain. The patient endured tremendous pain resulting from her bone cancer but held on until the graduation of her first son from secondary school. Bone cancer is particularly atrocious, and the patient implored the medical staff to grant her wish to die and bring an end to her pain. Petrus walked into the room and was confronted with the patient's wails and pleas for the respite of death. Here I am reminded of Nietzsche's powerful insight: "the final reward of the dead—to die no more" (Nietzsche, n.d. [a]). The nurses and doctors stayed away from the room because they had nothing more to offer. The patient had maxed out on her pain medication. Yet the patient asked for more. She asked for that final injection. They felt extremely helpless and looked to Petrus for help.

Upon entry into the patient's room, Petrus asked her how he could help. The patient straightforwardly asked Petrus to help end her life. She told him that she had waited long enough and that she did her part in hanging in there with the pain so as to be there for her son's graduation. However now she wanted to be "selfish" and wished to die. What to do? Similar to the medical staff, Petrus was also confronted with his own helplessness and desperation. Unsure how to respond, Petrus stayed with the patient while offering assurances that felt quite hollow. And seeing that they offered her little comfort, he, too, left the room after a short while.

Petrus came into supervision a few days later asking me what he could have done. Parallel process kicked in, for now I also felt the same helplessness. Typically, when dealing with anticipatory grief, we help our clients complete unfinished business and die with as little regret as possible. However, in this case, the patient had held on and completed her unfinished business of being present for her son's graduation. She lived up to her end of the bargain. Now her wish was to die. Being in the same boat as Petrus and the medical staff, I, too, was stupefied in my helplessness. How about you?

Drawing inspiration from the article Hanging In There, which I referenced in Chapter 3 of this book, I thought of a few things I had read near the time of the supervision. The first thing I thought of was courage—that it is our courage and not our degrees that earn the right to be our clients' therapist. We earn our client's trust because of our courage to enter into their suffering. The courage such as that Virgil the Roman poet displayed when guiding Dante through the nine circles of hell in the Divine Comedy by Dante Alighieri, widely considered to be the preeminent work in Italian literature. The question before Petrus and I was: Were we willing to enter into the hell that the client was experiencing and talk to her about death and euthanasia? Were we courageous enough to contemplate euthanasia with this woman in agony? And it began with whether I was willing to discuss euthanasia with Petrus during our supervision. Once again came the words of the end of the first verse of the Tao Te Ching: "Darkness within darkness, the gateway to all understanding" (Lao Tzu, 1995).

Bearing Witness

Shortly thereafter, the concept of "bearing witness" also returned to my mind; I was introduced to this term/concept while attending a recent conference. Bearing witness meant staying present and hanging in there amid our clients' suffering. Running away happens when we try to do too much; when we try to remove what cannot easily be removed, what should not be removed. Recalling Zhuangzi's parable of Flight from Shadow, referenced in the previous chapter, I endeavored to hang in there and bear witness to Petrus's suffering as he bore witness to his patient's suffering. For much of life cannot be explained, only witnessed (Remen, 2006, p. 299). This was no time for theory or causal explanations.

Bearing witness seems like such a simple concept that we are often left with the question, "Is it enough?" "Shouldn't we do more?" Do we just leave the clients there in misery and simply witness their suffering? But the therapeutic effect of bearing witness is not a standoff attitude as if we're simply an audience at a tragic play. Bearing witness is about compassion and companionship, being deeply present amid our client's suffering. It is our willingness to hang in there even though there is often nothing we can do to remove the pain. There is something powerful about hanging in when all we can do is to witness our clients' pain. When witnessed and seen, we communicate to our clients' that their pain and sacrifice matters.

Their existence is validated through our witness even though there is often nothing we can do to remove their pain, as illustrated by the Jewish Legend of the Lamed-Vov as told by Sheldon Kopp (2013). The Lamed-Vovs are thirty-six secret Just Men whom the existence of the world depended upon. When one dies, another takes his place. The only thing distinguishing Just Men from others is the heartbreaking depth of their compassion. The anguish of the Just Men is so inconsolable that even God himself is not able to give them comfort except to set forward the clock of the Last Judgment by one minute as an act of mercy. The story is told about a young boy who found out from his aging grandfather that he had been designated as one of the Lamed-Vovs. The boy was awed but overwhelmed as to how to fulfill his destiny. His grandfather informed him that there was nothing he needed to do except to be himself and continue being a good little boy.

But the assurances of the grandfather failed to alleviate the boy's burden. He was consumed with what it takes to be a Just Man and hoped that if he proved worthy, perhaps God would spare his grandfather from death. Thus, the boy began to imagine grand acts of torture and sacrifice that he could engage in to demonstrate his worthiness. The grandfather was deeply moved when he learned of the depth of the boy's love and sense of responsibility. He taught the boy the error of his ways by explaining that a Just Man will not be able to change anything:

> He will save no one. A Just Man need not pursue suffering. It will be there in the world for him as it is for each man. He need only be open to the suffering of others, knowing that he cannot change it. Without being able to save his brothers, he must let himself experience their pain, so that they need not suffer alone. This will change nothing for man, but it will make a difference to God. (Kopp, 2013, pp. 22–23).

The boy, being still a boy, was unable to understand how he could become a Just Man and save his grandfather and the world by doing nothing. His epiphany came later that day when he experienced deep empathy for the terror and helplessness of a fly that he captured with his hands. The fly's vulnerability was suddenly his own as well. Releasing the fly from his trembling hand, the boy suddenly felt the aurora of becoming one of the Lamed-Vov. He became one of the Just Men. He learned that "love is more than simply being open to experiencing the anguish of another person's suffering. It is the willingness to live with the helpless knowing that we can do nothing to save the other from his pain" (Kopp, 2013, p. 23).

Bolstered by these two important therapeutic attitudes, I found my direction and regained my footing. I invited Petrus to bring me into the patient's room with him. I asked him to reflect internally and describe for me as vividly as he could what it was like in that room with his patient. I then bore witness to Petrus' experience. I recorded what I heard. I opened myself up to the suffering that was in that room, both Petrus's and the patient's, and mirrored back to Petrus as deeply and faithfully as possible what I felt and heard.

Poetic and Pure Reflection

The concept of mirroring is simple to understand, but the quality of that mirroring makes a big difference. Early in our therapy training, we all learn about the importance of the basic skill of mirroring or reflection. But how do we go about it? What do we reflect? Content, process, cognition, affect, body posture, etc.?

For a long time, whenever I demonstrated role-plays, I tried to model the importance of listening to the music rather than the words. It's another way of valuing process over content. I instruct my students that it's important that we listen with all of our being and feel what the client is trying to communicate to us. Just as poetry is a tool, an avenue to communicate the inner self of the poet, the words that the client uses are also mere tools. It is their inner self, their being that we need to listen to and understand. Similarly, Rollo May (1994) illuminates, "the greatness of a poem or a painting is not that it portrays the *thing* observed or experienced, but that it portrays the artist's or the poet's vision cued off by his encounter with the reality" (p. 79). Therefore, we teach our students to focus not upon the words (content) but rather on the essence behind the words. So what we strive for is not simply content accuracy. Effective empathy is much more than content accuracy. What we strive for is ontological accuracy. We want to be aligned with and in tune with the rhythm, timbre, and melody of the client's being. And in this regard, poetry can be a powerful tool.

A good therapist operates much like an artist. The poet W.H. Auden stated that a poet "marries his language, and out of this marriage the poem is born" (as cited in May, 1994, p. 85). In the same book, *The Courage to Create,* May goes on to describe the creation process as an encounter that requires intense absorption on the part of the artist. He writes, "This intensity of awareness is not necessarily connected with conscious purpose or willing. We cannot *will* to have insights. We cannot *will* creativity. But we can *will* to give ourselves to the encounter with intensity of dedication and commitment" (May, 1994, p. 78). So instead of control, the artist must remain receptive. May's understanding of the creative process is an apt description for what it takes to properly bear witness and provide quality reflections or mirroring. In listening to Petrus's description of his experience in the room, I was not so much a reporter documenting his experience but more of an artist absorbed in the process, striving to listen with the third ear so I could poetically reflect on what was most poignant and moving in his narration. Just as a poet must be particular with his word choice, I, too, must be attuned to Petrus's and my experience and reflect the essence of those experiences. It is the difference between constructing an essay versus writing a poem.

I learned about the process of poetic reflection through a translation exercise. In fact, it was the translation of the Chinese song "Lilac," which is part of the narrative in the Chapter 3 that tells of Bruce's encounter through song. The lyrics from the song was beautiful and an intricate part of the story. Given my limited ability to translate Chinese, I asked a friend to make the initial translation. She offered a fine translation that matched the song nearly verbatim reflecting content accuracy. However, much of the essence of the song was missing. It failed to match the melody and capture the soul, the essence of the song. Those of you who have experience translating poetry will immediately understand. The original Chinese songwriter shaped the lyrics to fit that particular melody. It would have been very difficult to accomplish the same with a different language. Nevertheless, to do justice to the song and the story, I had to try.

Below you will find in the first column are the original Chinese lyrics. The second column is the more objective, verbatim translation conducted by my friend. The third column is my very subjective attempt to capture the essence of the song through what I consider to be a poetic translation. As you can see, my poetic translation took much liberty and was much looser. It portrayed my subjective understanding and feelings of that song. Objectively, it was a distant remnant of the original song. However, I believe the poetic translation offered a much closer depiction of the soul and message of the original song.

Original Chinese	Verbatim Translation	Poetic Translation
你说你最爱丁香花	You said your favorite flower is Lilacs	Your favorite flower is Lilac
因为你的名字就是它	Because Lilac is your name	For this is your name
多么忧郁的花	What a melancholy flower	A melancholic flower
多愁善感的人啊	What A sentimental person	A sentimental you
当花儿枯萎的时候	When the flowers are withered	Upon your wilting
当画面定格的时候	When the picture freezes	Time stood still
多么嫩的花	How many tender flowers	Such a tender and lovely flower
却躲过风吹雨打	Have dodged the wind and rain	Battered by the wind and rain
飘啊摇啊的一生	With the passage of a lifetime	Fluttering through life
多少美丽编织的梦啊	How many beautiful dreams have been weaved	Weaving dreams, one after another
就这样匆匆你走了	Just like this, you are gone	Hastily, you left
留给我一生牵挂	Leaving me a lifetime of concern	Leaving me a lifetime of reminiscence
那坟前开满鲜花	Fresh flowers fill the gravesite	Fresh flowers blooming at your graveside
是你多么渴望的美啊	How much beauty are you longing for?	The beauty you longed for
你看那满山遍野	See a whole mountainside	A mountain of blossoms
你还觉得孤单吗	Are you still lonely	Are you lonely still?
你听那有人在唱	Can you hear, there is someone singing	Listen, a serenade,
那首你最爱的歌谣啊	That song you love the most	your favorite ballad
尘世间多少繁芜	This world filled with needless words	Worry no more
从此必再牵挂	From now on, no need to be concerned again	About the needless cares of the world
(Repeat all x 1)		
日子里栽满丁香花	The day is filled with Liliacs	Lilac, my daily companion
开满制胜美丽的鲜花	Full of winning beautiful fresh flowers	My beautiful, blossoming Lilac
我在这里陪着她	I'm here to keep her company	I'm here with you
一生一世保护她	Protect her for a lifetime	to protect you now and forever

Though the poetic translation was quite challenging for me, I was very thankful for this teaching opportunity that fell across my lap. It helped me to demonstrate to students the difference between content and poetic reflection when it comes to reflecting what we've heard back to our clients. And paradoxically, less is more. Even though the poetic reflection offered fewer words/content and was therefore less objectively accurate, I believe it better captured the essence of the song. Fewer words added to the depths of its meaning. May (1994) teaches us that "creativity itself requires limits, for the creative act arises out of the struggle of human beings with and against that which limits them" (p. 113). Furthermore:

> Creativity arises out of the tension between spontaneity and limitations, the latter (like the river banks) forcing the spontaneity into the various forms which are essential to the work of art or poem. The struggles with limits is actually the source of creative productions. The limits are necessary as those provided by the banks of a river, without which the water would be dispersed on the earth and there would be no river—that is, the river is constituted by the tension between the flowing water and the banks. Art in the same way requires limits as a necessary factor in its birth.
>
> When you write a poem, you discover that the very necessity of fitting your meaning into such and such a form requires you to search in your imagination for new meanings. You reject certain ways of saying it; you select others, always trying to form the poem again. In your forming, you arrive at new and more profound meanings than you had even dreamed of. Form is not a mere lopping off of meaning that you don't have room to put into your poem; it is an aid to finding new meaning, a stimulus to condensing your meaning, to simplifying and purifying it, and to discovering on a more universal dimension the essence you wish to express. How much meaning Shakespeare could put into his plays *because* they were written in blank verse rather than prose, or his sonnets *because* they were fourteen lines! (pp. 113–114)

The other aspect regarding mirroring that I try to teach my students is that it is important that the reflection be pure and accurate, which requires that we bracket our assumptions, predisposing theories, and personal preferences. Bracketing is a central concept and the first step in the phenomenological method that is also known as the Rule of Epoche. Epoche is an ancient Greek term describing the state in which all judgments about non-evident matters are suspended. Thus, the concept of "bracketing" in mathematics is where we temporarily bracket or suspend a particular step while completing other steps in the calculation. Edmund Husserl, widely considered the father of phenomenology had a background in mathematics. In practicing Epoche, I was doing my best to suspend all beliefs and preoccupations, theoretical leanings, personal biases, hypotheses, previous knowledge or information, judgments, expectations, and assumptions in an attempt to understand as deeply as possible Petrus's experience in that hospital room with his dying client. I was doing my best to remain curious, open, disciplined, and naïve as I listened to Petrus's sharing.

Zen practitioners are very familiar with mirroring and the Rule of Epoche when they compare Zen consciousness to a mirror.

> The mirror is thoroughly egoless and mindless. If a flower comes it reflects a flower, if a bird comes it reflects a bird. It shows a beautiful object as beautiful, an ugly object as ugly. Everything is revealed as it is. There is no discriminating mind or self-consciousness on the part of the mirror. If something comes, the mirror reflects it; if it disappears the mirror just lets it disappear . . . no traces of anything are left behind. Such non-attachment, the state of no-mind, or the truly free working of a mirror is compared here to the pure and lucid wisdom of Buddha. (As cited by Merton, 1968, p. 6)

As long as we are trying to analyze, distinguish, judge, categorize, or classify, we are superimposing something else on the pure mirror. We are filling, rather than emptying. We are filtering the reflection through our preconceived paradigms, convinced that this will improve the reflection. It may indeed! But it is not pure reflection (Merton, 1968). Zhuangzi (2006) concurs when he wrote,

> The perfect man's heart is like a mirror.
> It does not search after things.
> It does not look for things.
> It does not seek knowledge, just responds.
> As a result, he can handle everything and is not harmed by anything. (Chapter 7, para. 27)

Our goal in therapy is to be that pure mirror, trying our best to put aside our assumptions so that we can come as close as possible to the client's own subjective experience. Thus, when my client shares with me the painful regret that she experienced about not being fully present for the brief time she was together with her father prior to his passing, if I'm practicing the discipline of Epoche, trying to be as clean a mirror as possible, I will then need to suspend my desire to soothe her pain and instead reflect back to her the subjective, painful reality of her experience. Now, this does not mean that my desire to soothe her pain or possibly offer an alternative view is not important; it simply means that to truly understand her subjective experience, it is necessary for me to suspend my personal view and desires in order to understand her experience as closely as possible from her internal world. Indeed, a mistake that we often make in such circumstances is to want to impose our views onto that mirror. Self-compassion and correcting distorted, overly harsh self-incriminating views are indeed critically important, but prematurely rushing into rescuing clients will often inhibit the client's natural path to healing. Transformation often requires going through the darkness. And once again, it is our willingness to enter into the darkness with our clients that will best help them to eventually see the light.

Thus, in order to bear helpful witness and accurately mirror back to Petrus his experience and the experience of his client that evening, I had to suspend my own feelings of helplessness, desire to assure Petrus that he did the best he could, concerns about getting in trouble for urging Petrus to risk talking about euthanasia with his client, my fear of appearing inadequate to Petrus, desire to teach existential theory, and empty myself to begin to record what Petrus told me as he shared his struggles.

Simple Translation: Wisdom from the Mouth of Babes

The paradoxical concept that limitation leads to creativity can also be found in the following additional lesson I learned regarding simple translations. I came upon the following children's story at the art exhibition of a friend of a friend in Taiwan.[1] The exhibition was the final class project of a remarkable art instructor who embodied the humanistic values of bringing the best out of his students through art.

---

[1] Facebook page for the art exhibition: https://www.facebook.com/pages/Buffet-11/425866020817799

He uses art as an affirming projective as opposed to the way that many clinical projective psychometrics such as the Rorschach and TAT are used these days to assess for psychopathology. His students will often find him inquiring, "I wonder what this part is saying to you?" Or, "why don't you explore this and see what you can come up with" when referring to a seldom-expressed part of the student's self that appeared on the canvas. The instructor was exploring possibilities as opposed to looking for pathology. The result of such nurturance was on display that evening. It was revealing for me to admire the progression and maturation of the students' artistic selves that were on display. The boldness and development of the students' expressions were easily discerned in the evolution of the paintings created as the class progressed. What was displayed was indeed the "healing arts."

As a final project of their choosing, several students opted to illustrate and write a children's book. Perhaps part of this choice is reflective of the fact that the art teacher helped each student to actualize their inner child. Upon hearing the following story, I was immediately touched and asked the author for her permission to translate it. The story powerfully illustrates many fundamental principles within existential psychology. Themes such as alienation, companionship, actualization, and authenticity were all powerfully present.

My initial thought was, this should be an easy translation. After all, it's a children's story. The story is not long and the words employed were quite simple. However, when I began the translation process, I found that it was arduous to convey what was most basic and pure. I was challenged to find simpler words to express beautiful, basic concepts and themes without resorting to jargon. Humanistic psychology's preference for simplicity can often be misunderstood as a lack of depth and sophistication. However, humanistic psychologists know that what is most simple is often what is most powerful and profound. I was translating a children's book, after all. I worked hard to avoid using familiar psychological terms such as transparency and authenticity. Think about it, dropping semantic bombs such as transience and ontology is a sure way to ruin a good children's story. So what I ended up with was a composite children's story in which I threw in a few fancy words. After all, how do you explain ephemeral to a four-year-old?

Nobel-prize winning researcher Daniel Kahneman (2011) offered the same advice if one wanted to come across as credible and intelligent. He advised against using complex language where simpler language will do. He quoted the work of his Princeton colleague Danny Oppenheimer, who showed that using pretentious language to express familiar ideas will often be taken as a sign of poor intelligence and low credibility. To serve as an example, the title of the article was "Consequences of Erudite Vernacular Utilized Irrespective of Necessity: Problems with Using Long Words Needlessly." Who are we trying to impress anyway?

The process of translating this children's story helped me to realize its parallel when it comes to supervision and therapy. The challenge of a good supervisor or therapist is to translate and simplify abstract psychological concepts for our supervisees or clients. Instead of mystifying therapy, humanistic psychologists strive to be simple and transparent. We strive to create intimacy rather than mystique. Translating the lyrics of the song and the children's story helped me to appreciate that the abstract terminology we employ has its place in scholarly circles. Yet when it comes to engaging and inspiring our clients in the therapeutic process, wisdom does indeed come from the mouth of babes. Children's stories speak to our hearts and lead us directly to the heart of the matter. Perhaps this is why children, young and old, will listen to them over and over again and remain engaged every time. So the next time you're struggling to communicate something simple and fundamental to your supervisees or clients, perhaps you can consider sharing a children's story. We're never too old to have another children's story read to us. Meanwhile, enjoy the following children's stories. The first was shared with me during a recent therapy session with a client who was struggling to accept herself. The second is the story I translated for my artist friend:

I Don't Know Who I Am!

Once upon a time, there was one called Ta.
Ta did not know who she was.
Therefore Ta went everywhere searching for herself.

One day, Ta met a lion.
Ta asked the lion, "Hello, who are you?"
The lion said, "I am a lion!"
Ta asked the lion, "Am I a lion too!"
The lion said, "Look at yourself, you are weak. Can you hunt? Can you maul an antelope?"
Ta felt ashamed and lost. Yet, Ta was also confused.

In her heart, Ta thought, "Look at me, feeble and weak. I am a nobody!"

One day, Ta met an eagle.
Ta asked the eagle, "Hello, who are you?"
The eagle said, "I am an eagle!"
Ta asked the eagle, "Am I an eagle too!"
The eagle said, "Do you have wings. Can you fly? How wretched. You don't appear to have wings and you can't fly!"
Ta began to feel sad and fearful. Yet, Ta was also confused.
Ta said to herself, "Look at me, I have no wings, how sad! I am a nobody!"

Ta continued to look for herself. But as time passed, she became more and more downcast.
With her head hung low, Ta discovered minnows swimming in a small stream.
Ta asked a minnow, "Hello, who are you?"
The minnow said, "I don't know who I am."
Ta asked the minnow, "I too don't know who I am. Are we alike?"
The minnow said, "Why are you not in here? How can you survive out of the water? Don't tell me you can't swim!"
Upon hearing this, Ta realized that she had nothing and was without talent. Ta began to feel a deep sense of loneliness and pain. Yet Ta was also confused.
Ta thought to herself, "Look at me, I can't swim. There is nothing I can do. I am a nobody!"

Ta was consumed with, "I am feeble. I cannot fly. I cannot swim. I can't . . ."
Nevertheless, she never ceased to inquire, "Am I a sloth. Am I a flamingo? Am I a snake? Why am I not an elephant?"
....

Ta never stopped searching.
Till one day
Ta chanced upon a sad fellow, and through the eyes of this fellow found herself.
And lo and behold, the sad fellow also found himself through Ta's eyes too!

Both were speechless, startled by their encounter!
Suddenly and despite themselves, they began hopping excitedly about!
Happy as can be.
The meeting of two lonely hearts, realizing that they weren't so wretched after all!

Day after day, Ta and his new friend found more and more fellows who also found themselves in the eyes of each other.
Eagerly, they asked them, "Who are you guys? Who are you really?"
They all responded, "We are rabbits. All of us are rabbits!"
Excitedly, they began hopping about, cheering and embracing to no end!
Slowly, Ta begins to discover that she has a pair of long legs, soft and light . . .
Ta was filled with joy!

One day in the future, Ta once again met up with a lion.
Ta greeted the lion and said, "Hello lion. I am a rabbit. Nice to meet you!"

喜欢你的这一刻起
Appreciating This Ephemeral You

1. 我和你从出生到现在，每一天，每一刻，都紧紧依偎在一起。
From the moment of birth till now, every day, every moment, we have never left each other's side.

2. 一起散步，一起发呆，一起掉眼泪
Strolling in sync, vegging together, crying as one.

3. 只不过，总令我感到着急的是，为什么你都一直长不大呢？
而长大的我，却开始不习惯那个还是小小的你。
It's just that, what always troubled me was why you won't ever grow up?
The mature me has become unfamiliar with this childish you.

4. 我担心长不大的你速度不够快。
所以，我刻意昂首阔步，把你远远地甩在身后。
I always worry that you won't grow up fast enough.
Therefore, I strut on deliberately ahead, leaving you far, far behind.

5. 我也担心大家会取笑长不大的你。
所以，我费尽心思把你藏起来，不让任何人发现。
I also worry that everyone will make fun of the childish you.
So I carefully conceal you, making sure you remain hidden from view

6. 都是你让我变得不完美了，我讨厌长不大的你！
You keep me from perfection, I hate this childish you!

7. 我决定把你关进秘密的角落，
假装你从来都没有存在过
I will hide you in a secret corner,
and pretend that you've never existed.

8. 正当我以为自己就要脱胎换骨的时候，
离开你的我，却一点也开心不起来。
Yet just when I thought I've been reborn,
I find that apart from you, I remain unhappy.

9. 我想念有你陪我一起散步......
自在的感觉会让我的脚步轻盈，而那才是我原来走路的姿态。
I long to stroll with you again . . .
Such ease allowing me to saunter light hearted, restoring me to my original gait.

10. 我喜欢有你陪我一起发呆......
想像的天空会充满许多梦想的泡泡，而那才是我一直感到幸福的画面。
I like it when we can veg out together . . .
Imagining a world of possibilities. That is when I feel most blessed.

11. 我需要有你陪我一起掉眼泪……
肚子里满满的泪水可以毫无保留地宣泄，而那才是我最能够放松的时候。
I need you to share my tears . . .

For when my heart filled with tears finds comfort and assurance, that is when I am most at peace.

12. 原来，我怎么可以没有你呢？
Therefore, how can I live without you?

13. 就在这一刻，我打从心底喜欢上你了。
是你，让我成为独一无二的我。
Thus, from this moment on, I loved you again from the bottom of my heart,
It's you who empowers me to be uniquely myself.

As a final example of the beauty of humor in simplicity, I offer you the following poem written by my colleague and good friend Michael Moats. In an effort to communicate his understanding of existential phenomenology to his students, he wrote the following poem regarding the essence of existential phenomenology: "I woke up today. And it was beautiful."

So following my own advice regarding the poetic and the simplistic, the following is what I heard and recorded during our supervision session that evening with Petrus:

In the midst of nowhere, neither here nor there
Inevitable, yet not forthcoming
Uncontrollable, letting go
Distant, yet close
Unforgettable

Close to something,
Helpless
Yelling, turbulent,
Intimate, not yet peaceful
The Hastening of Death
Life is short, make the most of lifelong dreams
Guilt resists dying

I then passed these phrases back to Petrus and asked when was the last time he had written poetry? He chuckled and informed me that it had been over 25 years. I asked him to go home that evening and write a poem describing his inner experience of being with his client in the hospital room earlier that week. The phrases were to serve as his seed material. Here is the poem that Petrus wrote. He translated it into Chinese himself:

Pain Without Suffering

Life is unknown.
Pain is inevitable.
Pain is our shadow! Ever closer through evasion.
Unwelcomed, Unforgettable,
Helpless, Guilt-Ridden
Life is short.
Only in the face of Death's confrontation,
its menace, its inevitability,
will we feel pain without suffering

痛而不苦

生命無常，我們有時不能避免要接受一些痛苦的事情。
它就好像我們的影子一樣！我們愈想遠離它，它就走得愈近！
痛苦的經驗是不能忘記的！但又不想回憶！
它會使你無助、內疚！
生命雖然是短暫的，但唯有面對死亡的恐懼，
死亡的威嚇，接受死亡，才不感到痛是苦的！

Encounter: Showing Up

My goal in prescribing the exercise was merely for Petrus to gain a deeper insight into his experience. I did not expect or advise him to take the extra step of sharing the poem with his client but that is exactly what he did. How do you think the client reacted?

At the following supervision session, Petrus informed me that he took the risk and shared the poem with his client. The client was calm, quiet, and surprised that Petrus returned for another visit. The tempest had blown over. This reminds me of the simple but profound consultation that I received from a colleague a few years ago. Another case of helplessness. I was struggling with a client who simply would not promise to refrain from committing suicide. I leveraged our therapeutic relationship and employed all of my training and experience to be of help to her. I showed my colleague the records of our correspondence, and my colleague agreed with me that I was both responsible and compassionate in my care for my client. This brought me much comfort but still left me with tremendous feelings of helplessness. Then my colleague shared with me that her supervisor told her that sometimes all we can do is to show up and the rest is up to the client. Simple words but yet powerful. It's an act of valor to show up in the midst of helplessness. We take showing up for granted, but sometimes it is a tremendous act of will. Petrus demonstrated tremendous courage by showing up again. He told me that "having done all that I could do for my client, the only thing left for me to do was to show up and leave the rest up to the client."

The client was surprised that Petrus returned, but even more surprised to learn that he returned bearing a gift. Petrus asked for permission and then proceeded to read the poem aloud to the client. He then left the poem by her bedside table. The client cried a few silent tears and gave Petrus a simple thanks. It was a poignant moment. Just as Daniel Gottlieb taught, the patient passed through her period of despair. It was certainly tumultuous. She went on to live a few more weeks.

What difference did Petrus make? It's difficult to say. Was there any measurable change in the client? Also difficult to tell, difficult to measure. What empirical evidence can we give as to therapeutic effectiveness? Who knows? At the very least, Petrus provided brief moments of companionship during the client's most difficult hours of despair. Through poetry, Petrus bore witness to the client's deep suffering. I did the same for Petrus during our hour of supervision. While we reached the limits of medical analgesics, I'd like to think that through his presence, courage, creativity, and companionship, Petrus helped to alleviate some of the patient's suffering. For "where systems and formulae end, existential psychotherapy begins" (Mendelowitz & Schneider, 2007, p. 322).

Beauty

This brings us to the question of how to conduct therapy and supervision and what makes therapy . During an interview with Jeffrey Mishlove on the topic/title of The Human Dilemma, Rollo May (2013) remarked that when a culture/society is in decline and has lost beauty, goodness, and truth, psychotherapy becomes more in demand. This raises the question for me as to how to think about therapy. How are we training our students to become good therapists? For the sake of argument, framing it dichotomously, are we teaching our students to conduct efficient therapy or therapy that appreciates beauty? Are these two characterizations dichotomous? I would argue that efficient therapy is not always beautiful and perhaps efficacious but beautiful therapy is most often "efficient" and efficacious. Efficient in the sense that if we can awaken and possibly transform our client's being, we are more likely to address the core existential issues and thus impact a wider range of the client's behaviors. While efficiency may be easier to define, beauty is much more subjective and difficult to capture. Dick Farson, a colleague of Carl Rogers, remarked on this issue when he shared about the challenge of researching the efficacy of encounter groups. In outcome studies he's conducted regarding the efficacy of sensitivity training groups, he points to the discrepancy between subjective self-report versus "objective" reports of others. Namely, members of sensitivity groups often will subjectively report significant meaningful experiences, yet those changes will often not show up in pre- and post-group psychological tests or third-party observational checklists. This brings up the question of what it is that we are measuring anyway with some of these objective psychometric instruments. Farson goes on to contrast an aesthetic versus a utilitarian view of psychotherapy. He argues that:

> One of the highest purposes that man has is the aesthetic purpose, to create moments where he can experience himself in new dimensions and that has worth in and of itself whether it has a lasting benefit or not. I think the things we value most in our lives, romance, sunsets, all of the aesthetic experiences are very seldom tagged with the burden "does it work?" Of course they don't work. It's not even an appropriate question. (Farson, 2013)

I would describe the encounter between Petrus and his client as a moment of beauty. During such moments, an existential shift often happens. Unlike some forms of efficient therapy that strive for targeted behaviors, the existential encounter strives for shifts in consciousness, shifts in the client's core, their ways of being. This once again harkens back to the lessons of my dance instructors, who prescribed fundamental, repetitive exercises that helped us to learn to move our core, our center of gravity located near the abdomen, as opposed to our outer limbs. In this manner of dance, the flowing movement of our outer limbs results from the natural outward extension of the core movement of the body's center mass. Most untrained observers focus mainly on the outer limbs and miss this point entirely. Nevertheless, even the untrained observer can tell the difference between the novice dancer who is simply emulating the movement of the arms and legs versus the accomplished dancer who dances out from their core.

Similarly, "life-changing therapy," a term coined by American existential–humanistic psychotherapist James Bugental (1999), is about seeking core movement instead of goal attainment. Instead of the outer attainment of goals, it's about internal shifts. Changes in the foundation, the core that underlies the conditioning and behaviors. In other words, getting at the root of the cause. What we strive for is increasing awareness, perspective, possibilities, and options. Such shifts are often small and incremental but much more enduring. Too often the case, without shifting the core and addressing root causes, the narrowly defined targeted behavior will return or morph into some other symptom that will once again bedevil the client. In dance, just as in martial arts and psychotherapy, there are no advanced skills, only skilled movement. We begin with a natural response, then let each body take the path of least resistance to solve the problem. The body will know where to go, how to flow. There are no wrong movements. The only mistake is not moving at all.

Thus, in addition to the typical ways of understanding therapy in terms of stages, I also share my experience and observations with my supervisees that therapy and life is a succession of moments. To live each one is to succeed. We toil and journey along in both life and therapy, doing our best to listen and understand. I call this tilling the soil. This constitutes the majority of therapy. However, if we can be grounded, attuned, and learn to appreciate moments of beauty, profound change can happen when we capture and realize such ephemeral moments. We cannot intentionally create such moments. Yet, we can put in our effort and adopt a spirit of humility and appreciation for beauty is always there for us to discover. In addition to encouraging my students to appreciate the stages that one goes through in life, I also encourage them to take on a different perspective and look beyond linear stages to be better attuned to the magical moments of transformation that await our discovery. Once again, it is often the deep encounters in the midst of such moments that affect the important changes that take place during therapy practiced from an existential–humanistic perspective. When clients reflect on their therapy, when we look back on life, what we recall and value are defining moments, not developmental stages.

Daniel Kahneman (2011) found that we have two ways of evaluating experiences of suffering and joy, and these experiences are illuminatingly contradictory. He conducted experiments with patients undergoing colonoscopy and kidney stone procedures while awake. The duration of these procedures ranged from four minutes to over an hour. He gave patients a device that asked them to rate their pain every sixty seconds to collect their moment-to-moment experience of suffering. At the end of the procedures, the patients were asked to rate the total amount of pain they experienced during the entire procedure. One might expect that the final rating would represent the sum of the moment-by-moment experiences. Or that having a longer duration of pain is worse than a shorter duration. If only life were so linear, predictable, and easily calculated. However, what Kahneman and his colleagues found was that the patients' ratings were best predicted by what he called the "Peak–End rule" consisting of the average of the pain experienced at the single worst moment of the procedure and at the very end. Studies in numerous other settings have confirmed the Peak–End rule. And this applies not only to our experience of suffering but also to our experience of pleasure. What we recall and how we make meaning have much more to do with moments rather than stages.

To phenomenologists, these findings do not come across as a surprise for we are meaning-making creatures. In the end, people do not view their life as merely the sum or average of all the parts. We make meaning through the stories we construct, and these stories are constructed from the significant moments in our lives. And chief among these moments is the end-point, how the story will ultimately turn out. As Victor Frankl (1985) reminds us, meaning ensures it cannot be pursued. A seemingly happy life without much pain may be empty. A seemingly difficult life dedicated to a greater cause may bring great joy. It seems that we favor moments of intense joy over steady happiness. Certain pleasures and what matters at the end can make enduring suffering worthwhile.

Moments of deep encounter are exactly what is valued by the theologian Martin Buber. He characterized such moments as I–Thou encounters. Buber (2011) explains that both individuals are forever changed after each precious I–Thou encounter. These moments defy prediction and control, hallmarks of empirical science. Therefore, if we are willing to let go, align, and surrender ourselves to greater beauty, we can open ourselves and trust that such transformative moments will inevitably occur. In the words of Victor Frankl (1988):

> Imagine a music-lover sitting in the concert hall while the most noble measures of his favorite symphony resound in his ears. He feels that shiver of emotion which we experience in the presence of the purest beauty. Suppose now that at such a moment we should ask this person whether his life has meaning. He would have to reply that it had been worthwhile living if only to experience this ecstatic moment. For even though only a single moment is in question – the greatness of a life can be measured by the greatness of a moment. (p. 51)

So while we cannot control and predict such moments of beauty, we can help our supervisees in a spirit of humility and awe be attuned to and surrender to the appreciation of beauty. Polly Berends (1983) wrote *Whole Child/Whole Parent,* a book on parenting that embraced many Taoist principles. In the chapter on beauty, she asked why it is that the study of beauty, art, and music is called art and music *appreciation.* Why not art enjoyment or analysis? Analysis has to do with our mind while appreciation has to do with our soul. *Appreciation* is much more than liking something. It involves understanding and valuing. It is synonymous with gratitude that goes beyond merely liking or being happy with the way things are on the surface. In true gratitude, we appreciate the significance of whatever presents itself to us. If so, then everything, good or bad, can be appreciated and potentially beautiful. Cultivating this type of appreciation requires humility, and it starts with ourselves as therapists and supervisors. True gratitude is not possible without humility; true humility is not possible without gratitude. Berends writes that the secret to appreciating beauty is not doing or having but seeing. We do not have to know how to do beauty, only to be aware of it. "We are not here to look good or to do good, but to see *and thereby be* good" (Berends, 1983, p. 243). Just as it is with parents, our tasks as supervisors are not so much about teaching our supervisees to do good or produce beauty. Rather, through a spirit of humility, together with our supervisees, be open to appreciating the possibilities that the healing power of beauty has to offer.

So once again back to Petrus and his client. Objectively, it was difficult to ascertain for certain what changes or shifts were gained by the client. However, I can share with certitude that both Petrus and I were changed, the evidence of which is in the words on this page. In the short duration of the client's stay in hospice, Petrus was able to provide a measure of companionship during the most intense period of the client's pain and despair. Given the peak–end rule, I'd like to think that

Petrus helped to lessen the client's suffering through his companionship during her darkest period of despair and that he made meaning of the suffering thereafter. It was significant that Petrus was there, and the gift of the poem, at the very least, helped Petrus and me to make meaning and feel more worthy of our suffering. We hoped the same could be said for the client as well at the end of her life. The beauty of what Petrus created ripples on. For at least one evening Petrus returned to poetry and returned to his artist within, while both of us learned more about courage and bearing witness.

I opened this chapter with a stimulating question and would like to end the chapter and the book with another question that proved to be inspirational. At the same time, I offer a poem of my own as a response to that question. The question has to do with the artist within, which I'd argue is true for all of us. It was posed by a participant at a workshop conducted in Shenzhen, located in southern China, following the Second International Conference on Existential Psychology in China. The topic of our workshop was Creativity and Existential Psychology. Louis Hoffman set the tone for the entire trip by sharing his poetry and educating the audience about the effective use and healing effects of poetry. This inspired one participant to share her own story. She shared that she was an artist but had given up her art to "face reality" and support herself financially. Perhaps another unspoken reason that she gave up her art can be deduced from her observation that many famous artists such as Van Gogh and Hemingway were tortured souls whom many considered to be mentally ill. She wanted our opinions about art and mental health. It was obvious that she was inspired by the workshop, yet faced the fear of returning to her art, if she could even find it again. She sought our guidance. I offered a response that contained the themes in the following poem. With the benefit of additional time and reflection, I've supplemented my response with the following poem of my own as I awakened to my own artist within:

Your artist within
has never left.
She is only asleep,
dormant in the deep recess
of your soul.

Is she calling to you?
Is she calling for you?
If so,

Say Yes,
Quickly!

What you've awakened to today
is not the absence of your artistry,
but the hibernation of your soul.

What you've awakened to today
is the joy of rediscovery,
coupled with the fear of isolation.
An awakening indeed!

What will you do?
How should you act?
How should we live?
How must we be?

Naïve questions one in all!

Who is crazy?
What do you say?

Craziness,
a prerequisite for treatment
East and West.
If so, let it be.

For who is crazy
and who is sane?
Those of us who travel
the road less travelled,
know better.[2]

The story of the artist within continued as the translator for our workshop sent me the following poem, her first, on her way to the airport flying back home after the workshop. She'd been captivated by existential psychology through attending our pre- and post-conference

[2] The poem was also inspired by Rumi and my friend and colleague Louis Hoffman.

workshops in addition to the main conference itself. She had studied literature during her university years but decided to abandon her dream to write and entered the world of finance because of family pressure. Yet her artist within had awakened as well, as evidenced by the following poem:

In the morning of the day,
I sit in the taxi that drives me
on the highway,
city skylined,
by the sunshine I can see
I feel life so free

I opened the car window
and take a deep breath of the freshness
the gentle mist quickly
disappeared in the sun
So no more worries
the direction is blurred.

Building and trees quickly set behind,
Still as I sat,
feeling flying high.
Many journeys I took before
assigned or given
I treasure this one chosen.

Even though time not abundant
I opened this book in my hand
The Psychology of Existence

References

Albom, M. (2009). *Have a little faith: A true story*. Hachette Books.

Alchemy. (n.d.). *Alchemy*. Retrieved January 27, 2017 from http://alchemyinc.net/stories-and-myth/

Berends, P. B. (1983). *Whole child/whole parent*. Harper & Row Publishers,

Brand, P. (1993). *Pain, the gift nobody wants*. Harper Collins Publisher.

Brooks, D. (2014, March). Should you live for your résumé—or your eulogy? [video file]. Retrieved from http://www.ted.com/talks/david_brooks_should_you_live_for_your_resume_or_your_eulogy

Brown, B. (2010, June). *The power of vulnerability*. [video file]. Retrieved from http://www.ted.com/talks/brene_brown_on_vulnerability

Buber, M. (2011). *I and thou* (W. Kaufman, Trans.). [Kindle for Android]. Retrieved from Amazon.com.

Bugental, J. (1999). *Psychotherapy isn't what you think*. Zeig & Tucker.

Caputo, J.D. (2006). *The weakness of God: A theology of the event (Indiana series, Philosophy of Religion)*. Indiana University Press.

Coehlo, P. (2006). *The alchemist* (A. R. Clarke, Trans.). Harper and Collins,

Chodron, P. (1997). *When things fall apart: Heart advice for difficult times*. Shambhala Publications, Inc.

Craig, E. (2000). *Self as such: Self, spirit, and the existing human*. Unpublished paper presented at the Old Saybrook 2 Conference, May 11–14. University of West Georgia, Carrollton, GA.

Dias, J. (2017). Wu wei. In Yang, M. (Ed). *Existential psychology and the way of the Tao. Meditations on the writings of Zhuangzi*. London: Routledge.

Farson, D. (2013, March 19). *1969 sensitivity training and encounter groups on public TV*. Charles K. Ferguson. [Video file]. Retrieved from https://www.youtube.com/watch?v=BKII2hrWLNM.

Fausset, H. L, (1969). *The flame and the light: Meanings in vedanta and Buddhism*. Greenwood Press.

Finkel, M. (2017). *The stranger in the woods: The extraordinary story of the last true hermit*. Alfred A Knopf.

Frankl, V. (1985). *Man's search for meaning*. Pocket Books.

Frankl, V. (1988). *The will to meaning: Foundations and applications of logotherapy*. Penguin Group

Franklin, B. (n.d.). Quotes from Ben Franklin. Retrieved from http://www.goodreads.com/quotes/372803-that-which-hurts-also-instructs.

Galloway, T. (1997). *The inner game of tennis: The classic guide to the mental side of peak performance*. Random House.

Gendlin, E. T. (1981). *Focusing*. Bantam Dell.

Gibran, K. (2015). *The prophet* [Kindle for Android]. Retrieved from Amazon.com.

Glotzer, L. (Producer), & Darabont, F. (Director). (1994). *The Shawshank redemption* [Motion Picture]. Castle Rock Entertainment.

Gottlieb, D. (2010). *The wisdom of Sam: Observations on life from an uncommon child.* Hay House.

Gu Chen. (2005). *Sea of dreams. The selected writings of Gu Chen* (J. Allen Trans). New Directions Publishing Corp.

Hafiz. (2006). *I heard God laughing: Poems of hope and joy* (D. Ladinsky Trans). Penguin Books.

Hafiz. (2010, March 2). *Libby Pink.* [Online Blog]. Retrieved January 31, 2016 from http://libbypink.com/2010/03/how-did-the-rose/

Hammarskjold, D. (n.d.). Quote retrieved February 17, 2016 from BrainyQuote.com: http://www.brainyquote.com/quotes/quotes/d/daghammars152627.html

Hardy, T. (n.d.). Quote retrieved January 18, 2015, from BrainyQuote.com: http://www.brainyquote.com/quotes/quotes/t/thomashard152301.html

Heider, J. (2005). *The tao of leadership: Lao Tzu's Tao Te Ching adapted for a new age.* Green Dragon Publishing.

Hess, H. (2012). *Siddhartha.* Harper Collins Publishers, Ltd.

Indiana School of Medicine, (2015, May 14). Commencement: Dr. Kent Brantly [video file]. Retrieved from www.youtube.com/watch?v=GaRz8YGaGQk

Inman, R. (2009, January 5). *Positive thinker's journal.* [Online Journal of Positive Thoughts and Inspirational Quotes]. Retrieved from http://positivethinkersjournal.blogspot.com/2009/01/teacher.html

Iyer, P. (2014). *The art of stillness: Adventures in going nowhere* (TED Books). Simon & Schuster, Inc.

Jackson, P., & Delehanty, H. (2013). *Eleven rings: The soul of success* [Kindle for Android]. Retrieved from Amazon.com.

Jacobs, P. (2015, April 16). *A Navy SEAL commander told students to make their beds in the best graduation speech of 2014.* Retrieved from http://www.businessinsider.com/mcraven-best-commencement-speech-university-texas-2015-4

Janssen, J. S. (n.d.). *The art of hanging-in there.* Retrieved from http://www.psychotherapynetworker.org/magazine/recentissues/2012-julyaugust/item/1743-the-art-of-hanging-in-there

Johanson, G. & Kurtz, R. (1991). *Grace unfolding: Psychotherapy in the spirit of Tao Te Ching* . Harmony Books.

Kahneman, D. (2011). *Thinking, fast and slow.* [Kindle for Android]. Retrieved from Amazon.com.

Kazantzakis, N. (n.d.). Quote retrieved from: http://www.goodreads.com/author/quotes/5668.Nikos_Kazantzakis

Kopp, S. (1972). *Guru: Metaphors from a therapist.* Science and Behavioral Books.

Kopp, S. (2013). *If you meet the Buddha on the road, kill him: The pilgrimage of psychotherapy patients* [Kindle for Android]. Retrieved from Amazon.com.

Kusher, H. (2004). *When bad things happen to good people.* Anchor Books.

Lao Tzu (1995). *Tao Te Ching* (S. Mitchell, Trans.). Retrieved May 2, 2019, from http://albanycomplementaryhealth.com/wp-content/uploads/2016/07/TaoTeChing-LaoTzu-StephenMitchellTranslation-33p.pdf

Lao Tzu, (2003). *Tao Te Ching: The definitive edition* (J. Star. Trans). Jeremy Tarcher/Putnam.

Lao Tzu, (2009). *Lao Tzu: Tao Te Ching: A book about the way and the power of the way* (U.K Le Guin. Trans). Shambhala Publications Inc.

Lao Tzu, (2012). *Tao Te Ching: Six complete translations* (I. Mears. Trans). Start Publishing, LLC.

Lin, Y. (2008). *The importance of living* [Kindle for Android]. Retrieved from Amazon.com.

Maugham, S. (2004). *The painted veil.* Vintage Books.

May, R. (1969). *Love and will.* W. W. Norton & Co.

May, R. (1981). *Freedom and destiny.* Norton & Co.

May, R. (1991). *The cry for myth.* W. W. Norton & Co.

May, R. (1994). *The courage to create.* W. W. Norton & Co.

May, R. (2013, March 19). *Rollo May: The Human Dilemma* (Part One Complete): Thinking Allowed with Jeffrey Mishlove. [Video file]. Retrieved from https://www.youtube.com/watch?v=HH-9XkjqYHY.

Mendelowitz, E., & Schneider, K. (2007). Existential psychotherapy. In *Current Psychotherapies* (Vol. 8). Thomson Brooks/Cole.

Merton, T. (1968). *Zen and the birds of appetite.* New Directions Publishing Corporation.

Merton, T. (2010). *The way of Chuang Tzu.* New Directions Publishing Corporation.

Misiak, H., & Sexton, V.S. (1973). *Phenomenological, existential, and humanistic psychologies: A historical survey.* Grune and Stratton.

Nietzsche, F. (n.d. [a]). Quote retrieved March 14, 2019, from goodreads.com: https://www.goodreads.com/quotes/882357-the-final-reward-of-the-dead---to-die-no

Nietzsche, F. (n.d. [b]). Quote retrieved January 13, 2017, from onelifeonly.net: http://www.onelifeonly.net/becoming-wise/

Nietzsche, F. (2008). *Thus spoke Zarathustra: A book for everyone and nobody.* [Kindle for Android]. Retrieved from Amazon.com.

O' Brien, B. (2016, April 6). *The Buddha's raft parable: What does it mean?* Retrieved February 16, 2016, from http://buddhism.about.com/od/sacredbuddhisttexts/fl/The-Buddhas-Raft-Parable.htm

Proust, M. (1993). *In search of lost time. The complete masterpiece* (C.K.S. Moncrief, T. Kilmartin, & A. Mayor, Trans). Random House.

Rajneesh, B. S. (1981). *Yoga* (Vol. 9) *The Alpha and the Omega.* Rajneesh Foundation. New York, NY.

Remen, R.N. (n.d.). Rachel Naomi Remen, M.D. website: Retrieved January 30, 2016, from http://www.rachelremen.com/about/

Remen, R.N. (2000). *My grandfather's blessings: Stories of strength refuge and belonging* [Kindle for Android]. Retrieved from Amazon.com.

Remen, R.N. (2006). *Kitchen table wisdom:* 10th anniversary edition [Kindle for Android]. Retrieved from Amazon.com.

Riis, J. (n.d. Quote retrieved from: http://www.brainyquote.com/quotes/authors/j/jacob_riis.html

Rilke, R. M. (n.d.). Quote retrieved from http://www.goodreads.com/quotes/119250-do-not-assume-that-he-who-seeks-to-comfort-you

Rogers, C. (1961). *On becoming a person.* Houghton-Mifflin Harcourt Publishing Co.

Rogers, C. (1980). *A way of being*. Houghton-Mifflin Publishers Inc.

Rumi, J. (n.d.). [Quote retrieved from http://thinkexist.com/quotation/silence-is-the-language-of-god-all-else-is-poor/763267.html

Saint Exupéry, A. (2000). *The Little Prince* (R. Howard, Trans.). [Kindle for Android]. Retrieved from Amazon.com.

Schulkin, D. (2014). A journey toward authenticity. In M. Heery (Ed.), *Unearthing the moment: Mindful applications of existential–humanistic and transpersonal psychotherapy* (pp. 140–147). Tonglen Press.

Spinelli, E. (1997). *Tales of un-knowing: Eight stories of existential therapy*. New York University Press.

Spinelli, E. (2005). *The interpreted world: An introduction to phenomenological psychology* (2nd ed.). Sage Publications. London. UK.

Storr, A. (1990). *The art of psychotherapy* (2nd ed.). Routledge.

Talmud. (n.d.). Quotes from The Talmud]. Retrieved from https://en.wikiquote.org/wiki/Talk:Talmud.

Terence. (n.d.). Quote retrieved January 18, 2015, from http://www.brainyquote.com/quotes/quotes/t/terence378795.html

Tillich, P. (1963). *The eternal now.* Scribner

Trenfor, A. K. (2014, February 5). *Philosiblog*. [Online Blog Article]. Retrieved from http://philosiblog.com/2014/02/05/the-best-teachers-are-those-who-show-you-where-to-look-but-dont-tell-you-what-to-see/

Vattimo, G. & Rovatti, P.A. (2013). *Weak thought: SUNY series in contemporary Italian philosophy*. State University of New York Press.

Viesturs, E. (2007). *No shortcuts to the top: Climbing the world's 14 highest peaks.* Broadway Books.

Watts, A. (1957). *The way of Zen.* [Kindle for Android]. Retrieved from Amazon.com.

Weixin, Q. (1949). *Essays in Zen Buddhism* (D. Suzuki, trans,). Grove Press.

Yalom, I. (1980). *Existential psychotherapy*. Basic Books Publishers Inc. k, NY.

Yalom, I. D. (1992). *When Nietzsche wept.* New York: Basic Books.
Yalom, I. (2002). *The gift of therapy: An open letter to a new generation of therapists and their patients.* Harper Collins Publishers Inc.
Yalom, I. (2008). *Staring at the sun: Overcoming the terror of death.* Jossey-Bass.
Yalom, I., & Elkin, G. (1974). *Everyday gets a little closer: A twice-told therapy.* Basic Books.
Yang, M. C. (Ed.). (2017). *Existential psychology and the way of the Tao: Meditations on the writings of Zhuangzi.* Routledge.
Zhuangzi, (1998). *Wandering on the Way: Early Taoist tales and parables of Chuang Tzu* (V. Mair, Trans.). University of Hawaii Press.
Zhuangzi, (2006). *The book of Chuang Tzu* (M. Palmer, Trans.) [Kindle for Android]. Retrieved from Amazon.com.
Zhuangzi, (2013). *The complete works of Zhuangzi* (B. Watson, Trans.). [Kindle for Android]. Retrieved from Amazon.com.

Index

absurd, 37-8, 101
actualize, 27, 28, 91, 140
  self-actualization, 46-7, 91, 140
apprentice, 13, 15, 19, 62-3, 113
authenticity, 20, 27, 33, 34, 59, 69, 140, 158
awe, 69, 71, 151

barista, 12, 13, 14, 44, 62-4
bearing witness, 15, 29, 36-40, 55, 98, 102, 121-2, 132-5, 147, 152
beauty, 1-3, 8-13, 15, 22, 35-7, 40, 52, 58, 68-9, 82, 86, 90, 94-5, 97, 99, 101, 103-4, 117, 119, 120, 122, 130-1, 135-6, 138, 140, 145, 147-152
bracketing, 75, 102, 137-8
Bugental, J. 5, 9, 149, 155

Camus, A. 37
Chuang Tzu. *See* Zhuangzi
companionship, 17, 20, 25, 28, 55, 56, , 82, 84, 92, 94, 109, 127, 129, 130, 132, 140, 147, 151
compassion, 38, 82, 85, 87, 93, 105-6, 107, 109, 121, 129, 132-3, 139, 147
  self-compassion, 85-7
Congruence, 54
courage, 1, 7, 10, 15, 21, 96, 98, 102, 109, 112, 121-2, 132, 147, 152, 157
creativity, 102, 110, 135, 137, 139, 147

darkness, 3, 24, 46-9, 65, 71, 89, 90, 98, 122, 132, 139
despair, 38, 96, 99, 106, 110, 122, 131, 147, 151
death, 18, 92-4, 100-1, 103, 105-8, 110, 119-23, 131-3, 138, 145-6

embodiment, 24, 33
empathy, 28, 33-4, 40, 59, 113, 115, 133-4
emptiness, 27-8, 55, 66, 75-7, 79-81, 84, 96, 101-2, 105, 107, 110, 115-8, 122, 124, 138-9
encounter, 5, 15-6, 20, 43, 46, 84, 99, 100, 102, 124, 134, 135, 143, 148, 150, 155
ephemeral, 9-10, 12, 114, 140, 149
eternal, 1, 3-4, 10-2, 24, 101-2, 119-120, 158
evil, 37, 39-40, 89-90, 98
existence, 3, 5, 6-7, 11, 16, 20, 24, 36-7, 39-40, 55, 72, 74, 77, 82, 84, 94, 102, 112, 133
existential Isolation, 82, 84

failure, 3-5, 16, 25, 45, 71, 86-8, 93
faith, 17, 20, 32, 62, 74, 86, 109, 155
focusing, 9, 61-5, 114-5, 124-5, 155
Frankl, V., 7, 38, 49, 77, 83, 105, 150, 155
freedom, 7, 9, 12, 16, 76, 91
fully present, 114-5, 139

Gibran, K. 32, 119, 123, 155
grace, 14, 42, 85, 99
gratitude, 12, 20, 101, 127, 151
grief, 39, 93, 119, 121, 130, 131, 165
guru, 1, 24-5
see master, sage

harmony, 25, 31, 61, 113
Hasidic, 1, 2, 25
helplessness, 6, 25, 38, 84, 96, 108, 110, 122, 128, 129, 131, 133, 134, 139, 146

impermanence, 43, 101
inspiration, 1, 7, 11, 15, 19, 25, 44, 100, 110, 122, 131, 132

Jung, C. 24, 40, 90

Khora, 30, 74, 80, 88
Kopp, S. 2, 45, 133

letting go 43, 49, 51

master, 1, 24, 45, 51, 59, 61, 72, 77, 79, 106, 111, 118, 124
see guru, sage
Maugham, S. 4, 6
May, R. 2, 76, 83, 89, 118, 127, 129, 134-5, 137, 147
meaning, 6-7, 24, 27, 31, 37-8, 46, 49-50, 73-5, 82-3, 89, 98, 116, 120-1, 123, 128, 130, 137, 150-2, 155
see purpose

midwife, 29, 30, 115
mirror, 60-1, 66, 138-9
mirroring, 77, 134-5, 137-9
mystery, 22, 29, 80, 98, 123
myth, 79, 155, 157

Nietzsche, F. 27, 54, 66, 98, 131, 157, 159

pain, 1-2, 6, 12, 15, 17, 30, 37, 39, 41, 43, 75, 82, 89-91, 93-4, 96, 98-9, 101, 107-8, 110, 122, 127-34, 139, 142, 146, 150-1
paradox, 5, 6, 58, 61, 63, 89, 95
parallel process, 32, 109, 121, 130-1
passion, 12, 14, 27, 73, 88
pause, 76-7, 101
perfect, 3, 6-7, 22, 59, 88, 90-1, 95, 144
phenomenology, 4, 75, 86, 138, 145
Plato, 30, 74
poem, 20, 118-9, 134-7, 145-7, 152-3
poetic reflection, 135, 137
presence, 22-3, 48-9, 54-5, 84, 95, 102, 109, 115, 130, 147
purpose, 13, 15, 44, 51, 74, 148
See meaning

Rajneesh, 42, 158
rebellion, 9, 10, 37, 38, 40
Remen, R. 22-3, 36, 115, 132, 158
resilience, 29, 85, 109-110
rippling, 7, 17, 20, 37, 64, 152
Rogers, C. 5, 40-1, 44, 59, 65, 86, 148, 158

sage, 21, 25, 56, 65-6, 97
see guru, master

Siddhartha, 52, 76, 156
simplicity, 8, 58-9, 116, 137, 140-1, 145
Sisyphus, 38
Socrates, 29, 30, 115
solitude, 28, 76
Spinelli, E. 24, 48-9, 75, 158
steadiness, 112
stillness, 33-4, 61, 66-7, 76, 101, 115-6, 156
subjective, 4-6, 53, 135, 139, 148
suffering, 37-40, 49, 73, 82-3, 93, 95, 99, 110, 127-34, 146-7, 150, 152
surrender, 71, 102, 150-1

Tao Te Ching, 3-4, 19, 25-7, 35, 50, 56, 77-9, 86-8, 98, 106-7, 117, 122-3, 132, 156, 157
teacher, 1, 24-5, 30, 32, 58, 85, 92, 113, 121, 123, 140, 156
techniques, 41, 44, 49-52, 58, 62, 95, 102
transformation, 10, 30, 75, 97, 101, 149
transience, 43, 68, 101, 140

uncertainty, 17-8, 30, 69, 73, 75
unconditional positive regard, 15, 87
un-knowing, 48, 65, 158

vulnerability, 6, 92, 130, 133, 155
water, 7, 25, 27, 45, 52, 57, 60-2, 65-7, 69, 71, 78, 96-7, 106, 112, 137, 142
Watts, A. 51, 53, 61, 80, 158
Weak Therapy, 72, 74

About the Author

Mark Yang, PsyD is a licensed clinical psychologist and co-founder and director of the International Institute of Existential-Humanistic Psychology (http://www.iiehp.org), whose mission is to promote Existential-Humanistic Psychology and provide counseling skills training to mental health professionals in Asia. He is actively involved in the training and supervision of psychology students from the existential-humanistic perspective throughout Asia. His professional interests include: existential-humanistic psychology, individual and group psychotherapy, grief and bereavement counseling, legal and ethical issues in clinical practice, and cross-cultural psychology. Dr. Yang is the editor of the book *Existential Psychology and the Way of the Tao: Meditations on the Writings of Zhuangzi*. He is also the co-editor of the books *Existential Psychology: East-West* (Volume 1 & 2). Dr. Yang was born in Taiwan and immigrated to the United States when he was nine years old. He is also a dog and cat lover.

www.ingramcontent.com/pod-product-compliance
Lightning Source LLC
Chambersburg PA
CBHW070920270326
41927CB00011B/2648
* 9 7 8 1 9 3 9 6 8 6 6 5 7 *